101 GUITAR TIPS

STUFF ALL THE PROS KNOW AND USE

BY ADAM ST. JAMES

To access audio visit:
www.halleonard.com/mylibrary

Enter Code
2834-4082-8699-9654

ISBN 978-0-634-05341-2

HAL•LEONARD®
CORPORATION
7777 W. BLUEMOUND RD. P.O. BOX 13819 MILWAUKEE, WI 53213

In Australia Contact:
Hal Leonard Australia Pty. Ltd.
22 Taunton Drive P.O. Box 5130
Cheltenham East, 3192 Victoria, Australia
Email: ausadmin@halleonard.com

Visit Hal Leonard Online at
www.halleonard.com

TABLE OF CONTENTS

THE WHOLE NECK MAPPED OUT

Most guitarists spend their entire musical life soloing out of just one or two scale patterns, typically at the fifth and twelfth frets, depending on whether they're playing in the key of A or E. How boring that is for the listener, and really, how boring that must be for the guitarist. There are only seven different scale patterns that cover the entire neck of the guitar in any key. Learning them all is not only easy; it's mandatory for anyone who wants to develop into more than your typical hack lead guitarist.

Once you know the seven patterns, all you have to do is slide them up and down the neck to play in any other key. Remember that if you slide one of the patterns up two frets, you must slide all of the patterns in that key up two frets—they work together.

And even better, when you learn the seven patterns in one key, you've actually learned two keys—one major and one minor—because of the theory of relative majors and minors (see tip #12 for more).

These seven scale patterns are labeled based on the first note on the low string of each pattern and its relation to the root note C. So the pattern that begins on C at the eighth fret on the sixth string is "Pattern One." Each of the other patterns correlates with a scale step in the key of C major, so the pattern that begins with the open low E string is actually "Pattern Three," because it begins on E, the third step in the C major scale. For more on the scale numbering system, see tip #2. This method will make transposing to other keys easier and will aid in learning the notes in each key.

Here are the seven scale patterns in the key of C major/A minor:

TRACK 1

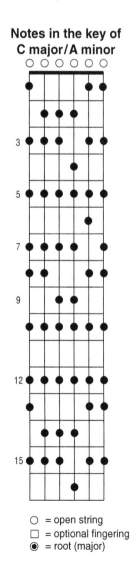

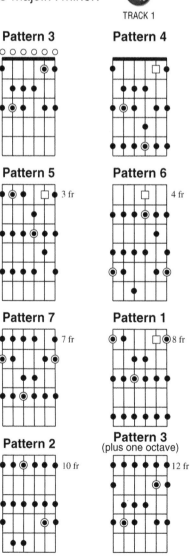

2 SCALE NUMBERING SYSTEM

If you've heard other players referring to mysterious creatures such as a "flat seventh," "two-five-one," or "sixth intervals," and don't know what they're talking about, you need to find out quick. This simple chunk of knowledge will help your entire understanding of not only the guitar, but of music itself. Here's the lo-wown: The notes, or "steps," of any scale—major, minor, modal, whatever—are often referred to by number, or by "interval" name (which is based on the scale step number). This numbering system then carries over into the naming of chords, chord progressions, and more. For example, the chord designation C7 indicates the chord has the flat seventh note of the C scale on top of a regular C chord. A simple blues or rock song based on the familiar I–IV–V (one-four-five) chord progression includes chords built on the first (I), fourth (IV), and fifth (V) scale steps of the chosen key. (Musicians commonly use Roman numerals when defining chord progressions—for more on this subject, see tip #7.)

The numbers of the scale steps (and interval names, such as "major third") are the same regardless of the key, as long as it's a major key. Here is a C major scale, with the numbers and interval names of the scale steps:

C major scale

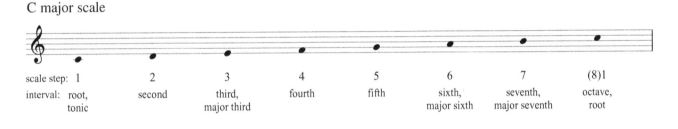

scale step:	1	2	3	4	5	6	7	(8)1
interval:	root, tonic	second	third, major third	fourth	fifth	sixth, major sixth	seventh, major seventh	octave, root

Numbering works the same with a minor scale or key, but the interval names change in some cases. Again, regardless of key, all minor keys have the same sequence of scale steps. Here is an A minor scale:

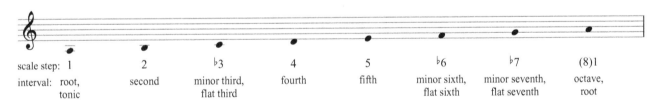

scale step:	1	2	♭3	4	5	♭6	♭7	(8)1
interval:	root, tonic	second	minor third, flat third	fourth	fifth	minor sixth, flat sixth	minor seventh, flat seventh	octave, root

A minor scale

To understand all the possibilities of number and interval names you might some day encounter, especially if you play modally or use extended or altered chords (such as a minor 7♭5 chord), you'll want to analyze a chromatic scale. A chromatic scale includes all twelve notes in one octave. Here is a C chromatic scale:

C chromatic scale

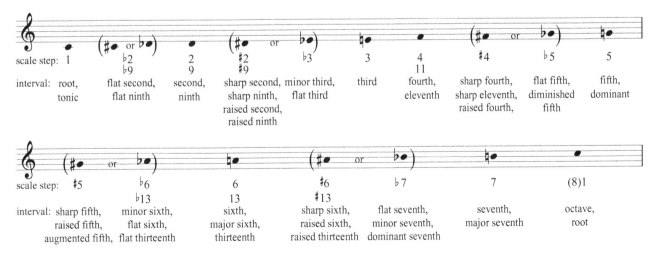

scale step:	1	♭2 ♭9	2 9	♯2 ♯9	♭3	3	4 11	♯4	♭5	5
interval:	root, tonic	flat second, flat ninth	second, ninth	sharp second, sharp ninth, raised second, raised ninth	minor third, flat third	third	fourth, eleventh	sharp fourth, sharp eleventh, raised fourth,	flat fifth, diminished fifth	fifth, dominant

scale step:	♯5	♭6 ♭13	6 13	♯6 ♯13	♭7	7	(8)1
interval:	sharp fifth, raised fifth, augmented fifth	minor sixth, flat sixth, flat thirteenth	sixth, major sixth, thirteenth	sharp sixth, raised sixth, raised thirteenth	flat seventh, minor seventh, dominant seventh	seventh, major seventh	octave, root

3 HALF STEPS AND WHOLE STEPS

Musicians of all types often refer to half steps and whole steps. These are essential building blocks for all types of music. Fortunately, you'll learn to hear them almost as quickly as you can learn what they are. A *half step* is two notes that are one fret apart, such as E–F or B–C. A *whole step* is two notes that are two frets apart, such as G–A or C–D. That's it. Drill the sounds of half steps and whole steps into your brain by trilling on them—playing a rapid series of hammer-ons and pull-offs on each variety until their sound is immediately recognizable to you at any time.

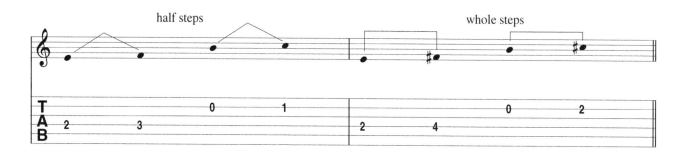

Also notice that half steps fall between the third and fourth notes of a major scale, as well as the seventh and eighth. The formula for a major scale could be written "whole-whole-half-whole-whole-whole-half." In a minor scale, the half steps fall between the second and third and the fifth and sixth notes of the scale. The formula for a minor scale could be written "whole-half-whole-whole-half-whole-whole." These formulas of half steps and whole steps hold true for all major and minor scales.

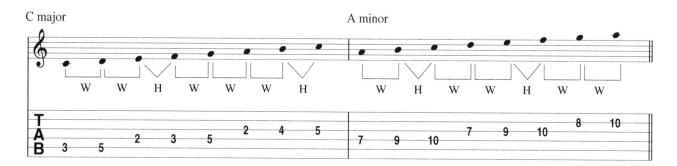

MODAL MADNESS

Everyone talks about modes, but how many really understand them? And how many really understand how easy it is to work them into their playing? Modal playing is quite common in Western music—that is, music emanating from the "Western" world, which is everything in every musical genre pouring out of North America, Western Europe, Australia, etc., as opposed to the exotic-sounding, semi-tone related stuff that is popular in Eastern Europe, India, the Middle East, and in traditional Chinese and Japanese music. (For exotic scales, see tip #64.)

Here's a quick primer on modes: If you're playing a song containing primarily chords built from the C major scale (C–Dm–Em–F–G–Am–B°), you'll use the same exact C major scale patterns, at the exact same frets described in tip #1, and this is what you'll be doing:

- If the song is based in C and keeps returning to the C major chord as its "home base" or "tonic," you're playing, obviously, in C major (a.k.a. C Ionian).

- If the song is based in D and keeps returning to the D minor chord as its tonic, you're playing in D Dorian. You'll have to shift your thinking: Play the same C major patterns, but treat the note D as the root note.

- If the song is based in E and keeps returning to the E minor chord as its tonic, you're playing in E Phrygian. You'll play the C major patterns, but treat the note E as the root.

- If the song is based in F and keeps returning to the F major chord as its tonic, you're playing in F Lydian. You'll play the C major patterns, but treat the note F as the root.

- If the song is based in G and keeps returning to the G major or G dominant seventh chord as its tonic, you're playing in G Mixolydian. You'll play the C major patterns, but treat the note G as the root.

- If the song is based in A and keeps returning to the A minor chord as its tonic, you're playing in A Aeolian. You'll play the C major patterns, but treat the note A as the root.

- If the song is based in B and keeps returning to the B diminished or B minor seven flat-five chord as its tonic—or if the B chord is played as any other type of chord (major, minor, extended, or altered), but the remainder of the song contains the same chords built from the C major scale as listed above— you're playing in B Locrian. You'll play the C major patterns, but treat the note B as the root.

Here's a quick-reference diagram that'll make mode selection easy, no matter what your tonal center or key:

modes

Ionian (Major)	Dorian	Phrygian	Lydian	Mixolydian	Aeolian (Natural Minor)	Locrian
C	D	E	F	G	A	B
D♭ (C♯)	E♭ (D♯)	F (E♯)	G♭ (F♯)	A♭ (G♯)	B♭ (A♯)	C (B♯)
D	E	F♯	G	A	B	C♯
E♭	F	G	A♭	B♭	C	D
E	F♯	G♯	A	B	C♯	D♯
F	G	A	B♭	C	D	E
F♯ (G♭)	G♯ (A♭)	A♯ (B♭)	B (C♭)	C♯ (D♭)	D♯ (E♭)	E♯ (F)
G	A	B	C	D	E	F♯
A♭	B♭	C	D♭	E♭	F	G
A	B	C♯	D	E	F♯	G♯
B♭	C	D	E♭	F	G	A
B	C♯	D♯	E	F♯	G♯	A♯

keys

5 REAL ROCK & BLUES SOLOING

Contrary to popular belief, the minor pentatonic scale we all learned early on is not the basis of most rock and blues solos—or not exactly. From Hendrix to Van Halen to just about everybody before and after, more rock soloing has been done in the Mixolydian mode than just about any other scale—that, and a hybrid that actually blends our old standby, the pentatonic (actually, the equally familiar six-note-per-octave blues scale), with the major-dominant sounding Mixolydian mode. Riff around awhile with the pattern shown at right, which I refer to as the *Mixo-Blues scale.* (Shown in A, it begins at the 3rd fret, but it's really based around 5th position.) You'll recognize it immediately. Try the sample riffs at different tempos, then play them over the rhythm track shown.

The Mixo-Blues pattern in A

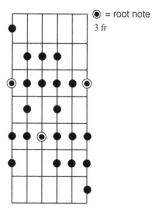

TRACK 2

TRACK 3 **Sample Mixo-Blues Riffs in A**

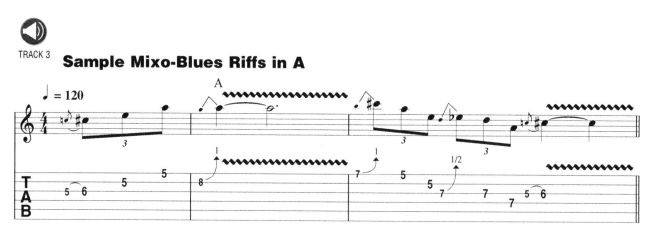

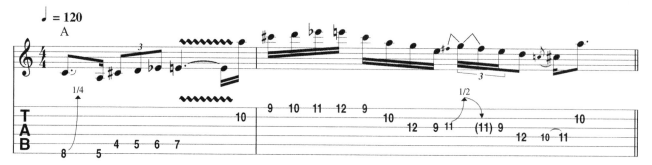

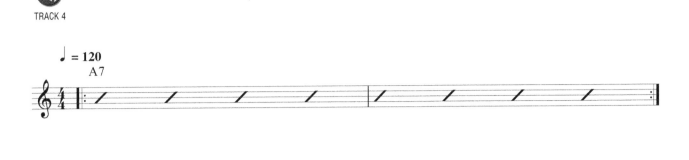

This is the same rhythm track for you to practice with.

$\downarrow$ = 120

A7

6 SATCH'S DRONE TONES

Joe Satriani taught me this excellent practice routine: Pick your low string once and let it ring for as long as possible while you play melodies or solo using the other strings on your guitar. If you're playing a regular six-string guitar tuned to standard tuning, your low string is an E. Start by playing your favorite solo patterns in the key of E, such as the minor pentatonic at the twelfth fret, or the Mixo-Blues scale described in tip #5. When your low string stops ringing, pick it again, then begin to solo using a completely different type of scale or mode, such as E Phrygian (which happens to be the same as C Major, conveniently diagrammed for you in tip #1). Then do it again using another type of scale, such as E diminished or the E whole tone scale or some really cool exotic scale that sounds like it came out of the Middle East (see tip #64).

The goal here it two-fold: First, you'll find cool riffs that just fall right under your fingers in different places on the neck using every scale or mode you ever learn. And second—and perhaps more importantly—you'll learn the different "flavors" of sound available to you when you know how to play using more than one or two simple scales. This might be the easiest practice method you'll ever find to expand your tonal horizons. And to make it even easier, we've recorded drone tones for you to solo over in all 12 tonalities (A, A#/B♭, B, C, C#/D♭, D, D#/E♭, E, F, F#/G♭, G, and G#/A♭—in that order). Have fun!

THE NASHVILLE SYSTEM

Novice players are often amazed when they are jamming with an experienced player who seems to be able to learn a song on the spot, often even before the song is over. Many times the more experienced player is able to do this because they recognize a common chord pattern, and regardless of the key, they know where the chord changes are going even before they get there. This is easily done once you learn the simple "Nashville" chord numbering system (and after you've learned enough songs to recognize some of the most common patterns). How Nashville got credit for something that's probably been going on since the days of Beethoven I don't know, but it probably has something to do with all the phenomenal studio players down there.

The chord numbering system brings us right back to basic scale numbering (see tip #2), because the chords and scale steps have the same numbers in any given key (hence the phrase "chord scales").

If you're playing a song in the key of C major, for example, C is the I chord (we use upper-case Roman numerals to indicate major chords, lower-case Roman numerals to indicate minor chords). And in the key of C major we would also have the following chords: D minor (ii), E minor (iii), F major (IV), G major (V), A minor (vi), and B diminished (vii°).

Chords in the key of C major

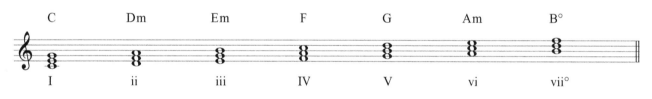

Things are only slightly different in a minor key. Let's look at A natural minor (which uses the same chords as C major, being the relative minor). The key of A natural minor would include A minor (i), B diminished (ii°), C major (III), D minor (iv), E minor (v), F major (VI), and G major (VII). When playing in a minor key, it is very common to change some of the minor chords in the progression to major chords. In particular, you might do this with the iv chord and the v chord (making D and E major chords, instead of minor chords, in the key of A minor). Changing these chords is really the result of a modal thing, but don't worry about that now.

Chords in the key of A minor

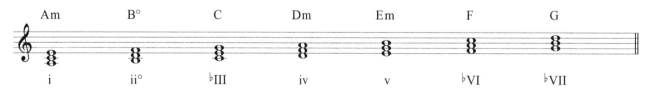

Also, if you're looking at a chart, you'll often see chords notated with the Roman numerals as shown above, but with a "7" after them, such as IV7 or V7. This indicates that the chord to be played is the dominant seventh variety of that chord. The V (five) chord in almost any song is played as a dominant seventh chord.

Here are a few very common chord progressions in major/dominant and minor keys. Using the numbering system, I'll also show you how to transpose a couple of these progressions as well. After that, I'll leave it up to you. No matter what style of music you play, you will recognize these chords patterns. Transpose away!

Common major progressions:	Key of C:	Key of D:
I–vi–ii–V–I	C–Am–Dm–G–C	D–Bm–Em–A–D
I–iii–IV–V–I	C–Em–F–G–C	D–F♯m–G–A–D
I–IV–V–I	C–F–G–C	D–G–A–D
♭VII–IV–I	B♭–F–C	C–G–D

Common minor progressions:	Key of Am:	Key of Bm:
i–iv–v–i	Am–Dm–Em–Am	Bm–Em–F♯m–Bm
i–iv–V	Am–Dm–E	Bm–Em–F♯
i–IV–V	Am–D–E	Bm–E–F♯
i–♭VII–♭VI–♭VII–i	Am–G–F–G–Am	Bm–A–G–A–Bm
i–♭III–IV	Am–C–D	Bm–D–E

TRANSPOSING

I spent a lot of my life playing original music, so transposing wasn't much of an issue. But now I spend a lot of my nights performing cover tunes in clubs, sometimes backing a singer or soloist.

Occasionally, the singer will want to play a song I might know, but in a different key than I usually play it in. Changing keys, or "transposing," is pretty simple with a three-chord blues or rock song. But start throwing in a few more chords, or an arrangement that includes a complicated bridge or musical interlude, and I have to start actually thinking about the chords and notes I'm playing or I inadvertently revert back to my original (wrong) key, and next thing you know, I'm out of a job. Quick, on-the-spot transposing requires knowledge of the Nashville numbering system described in tip #7.

To explain transposing, let's use a song with a verse that goes A–C–D, a pre-chorus that goes F–G–A, a chorus that goes E–D–A, and a bridge that goes C–B–A–E–G.

TRACK 6

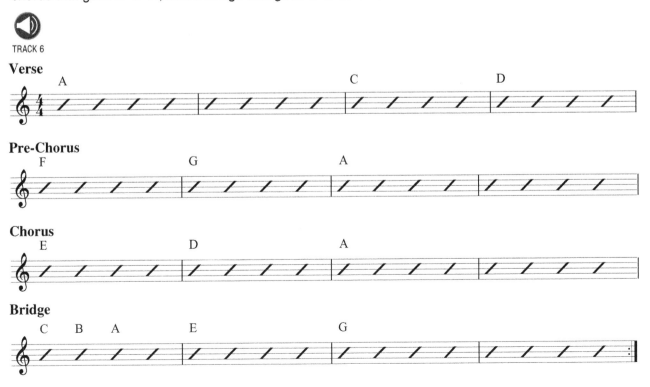

The song is in the key of A, but let's transpose it up a few steps to C. (We've used all major chords, designated by upper-case Roman numerals, to make this example quick and easy.)

Using the Nashville Numbering System, we'll first chart out the song as follows:

Verse	‖ I				♭III		IV	‖
Pre-Chorus	‖ ♭VI		♭VII		I			‖
Chorus	‖ V		IV		I			‖
Bridge	‖ ♭III II I	V		♭VII			:‖

Now we'll forget about the chord names in the key of A and just look at the chord *numbers* (the Roman numerals), and replace them with the appropriate chords in the key of C. Here's the same song, now charted out in the key of C.

TRACK 7

Verse	‖ C				E♭		F	‖
Pre-Chorus	‖ A♭		B♭		C			‖
Chorus	‖ G		F		C			‖
Bridge	‖ E♭ D C	G		B♭			:‖

Make sense? It may help to refer to the following Transposition Chart, which shows you the notes of all 12 major keys, and their respective Roman numerals.

Transposition Chart

I	II	III	IV	V	VI	VII
C	D	E	F	G	A	B
D♭ (C♯)	E♭ (D♯)	F (E♯)	G♭ (F♯)	A♭ (G♯)	B♭ (A♯)	C (B♯)
D	E	F♯	G	A	B	C♯
E♭	F	G	A♭	B♭	C	D
E	F♯	G♯	A	B	C♯	D♯
F	G	A	B♭	C	D	E
F♯ (G♭)	G♯ (A♭)	A♯ (B♭)	B (C♭)	C♯ (D♭)	D♯ (E♭)	E♯ (F)
G	A	B	C	D	E	F♯
A♭	B♭	C	D♭	E♭	F	G
A	B	C♯	D	E	F♯	G♯
B♭	C	D	E♭	F	G	A
B	C♯	D♯	E	F♯	G♯	A♯

Once you've determined a song's key, translate its chords into Roman numerals, and then into the chords of the new key. Some chords aren't in the chart above—like the ♭III, ♭VI, and ♭VII (in the key of C, the chords E♭, A♭, B♭); just flat (or sharp) the respective scale degree to get the desired chord.

Got it? Good. Now go use it before you forget.

9 TWO-FIVE-ONES

If there is a simple turnaround that you must know, it's ii–V–I (two-five-one). If you're in the key of A, that means B minor to E (probably E7) to A. In the key of E, it's F# minor to B(7) to E. If you don't understand the Roman numerals ii–V–I and how they relate to music, read tip #7.

The ii–V–I works in almost any genre, but it is absolutely, positively, required for jazz players. Not only should you master a variety of basic ii–V–I chordal turnarounds, you should learn how to solo over a ii–V–I as well, without mucking it up with inappropriate single-note riffs and hacked-up arpeggios. Of course, if you just don't know what to do as those chords go whizzing by, take B.B. King's advice on the topic: Grab one note and hold onto it (and bend as necessary) over all the mystery chords, taking off again when you find your place.

Some chordal ii–V–I's for inspiration

TRACK 8

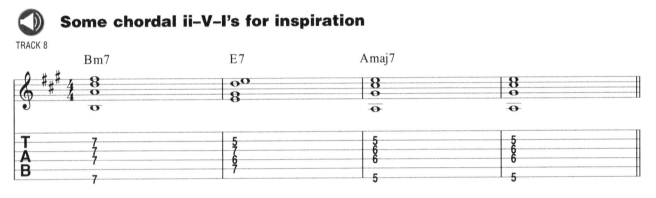

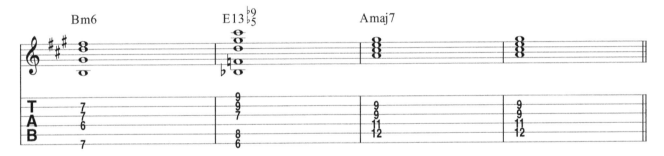

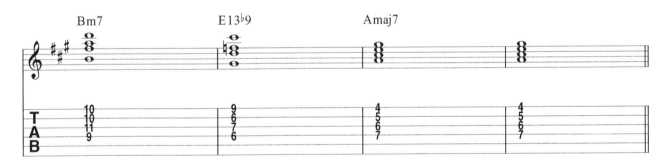

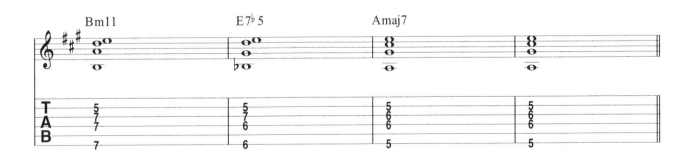

A few ii–V–I solo lines

TRACK 9

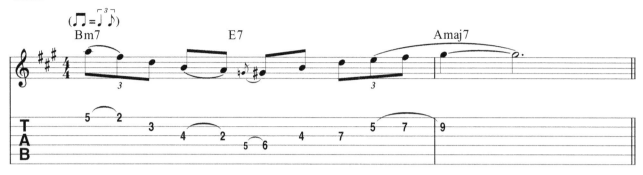

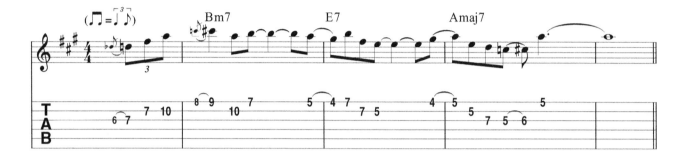

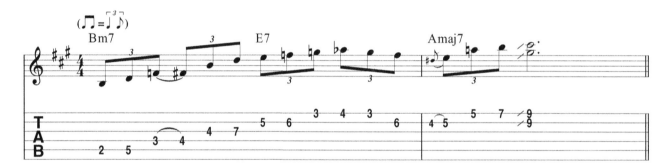

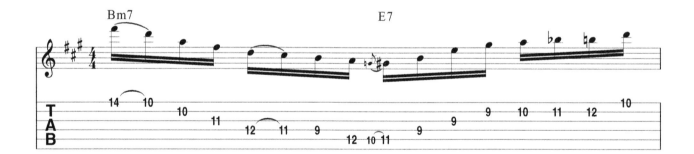

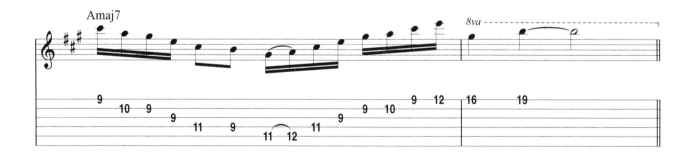

14

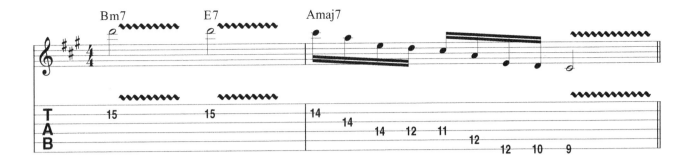

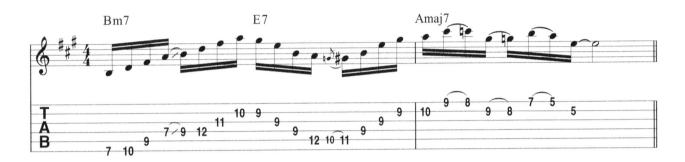

Here's the ii–V–I track minus the guitar for you to practice your own turnarounds and solo lines.

TRACK 10

 ONE-SIX-TWO-FIVE

OK, I said ii–V–I's were excellent, if not required, for many musical genres. If you've got a few of those under your belt, you're ready to get a little fancier. The I–vi–ii–V (one-six-two-five) progression is obviously just an extension of the ii–V–I, but it's a pretty cool extension, used by the best jazz, blues, country, and rock players—and especially songwriting masters such as Lennon and McCartney. These chord changes are useful either as quick turnarounds, or in a longer, drawn out section of a song. Try these on for size:

I–vi–ii–V progressions in various genres

TRACK 11

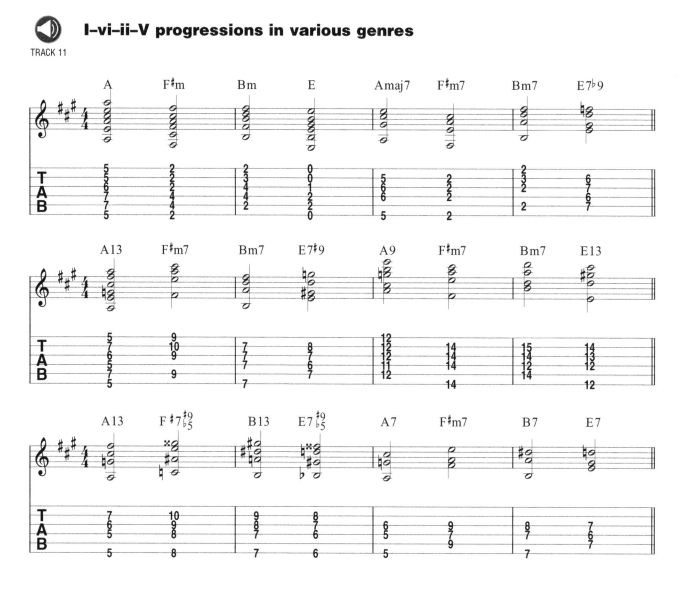

TRACK 12

Here's the I–vi–ii–V track minus the guitar for you to practice your own turnarounds and solo lines.

11 LEARNING BY EAR

When you're learning to play a piece of music by ear—such as a new hit song by your favorite recording artist—there are a couple of things to focus on to make learning easier.

First, listen for the song structure. Determine in what order each different section of the song is placed. This is referred to as the "arrangement." Musicians typically give these sections names such as intro, A section, B section, C section, chorus, bridge, instrumental break, or outro. Does the intro repeat at the outro? Is there a bridge or "middle eight," or just a verse and chorus? Is the solo over the verse progression or the chorus progression, or is it a new section altogether? Are there two different verse sections and a chorus section? Write the arrangement down if it makes it easier to learn (drummers use arrangement notes all the time). New and difficult songs are usually less intimidating when you see that most parts of the song are repeated numerous times.

Second, listen to and even learn the bass line, especially if you're having trouble figuring out the chords. The bass line will usually indicate which chords the guitarist is playing. Bassists typically focus on the "root" note of each chord and may also hang on the 3rd and 5th of the chord as well. (For more on scale and chord tones, see tip #2 and tip #16.)

For example, if the bassist is playing an A note for four measures, or even if he or she is riffing, but keeps hitting an A note, especially on the first beat of each measure, chances are the guitarist is playing an A chord. That A note, however, could also serve as the major 3rd of an F chord, the minor 3rd of an F#m chord, or the 5th of a D chord. You might need to experiment with different voicings and extensions of chords before you find the right one, but the bass line will be an invaluable tool in narrowing down your choices.

12 WHEN IN DOUBT, PLAY I–IV

It's almost impossible to overstate how common the I–IV (one-four) chord progression is in Western music. From the jazz and blues of the early twentieth century, to classic rock legends such as the Beatles and the Stones, right on through to the aggressive rock sounds of the twenty-first century, the I–IV chord change dominates the music we hear and play, particularly during the verses of a song. If you get lost during a song, try the I chord. If that doesn't sound right, try a IV chord. In the key of A, that would be the A and D chords, respectively. If it's neither of those chords, just wait, the band will get back to one of those two chords sooner than you think, and hopefully you'll be able to keep up after that. (And after I and IV, the next most common chord in most songs is V.)

If you can't remember which chords are I and IV in the key you're playing, think of it this way: Using an open E chord and an open A chord, the E is I and the A if IV. As you slide the E- and A-shaped barre chords up the neck, that relationship remains the same. So your standard rock 'n' roll A barre chord at the fifth fret and your standard rock 'n' roll D barre chord at the fifth fret will be I and IV, respectively.

13 RELATIVE MAJOR AND MINOR

Through the trickery of mathematics—and music and mathematics are very closely related—every major key has its relative minor key, and vice-versa. Go ahead, say it: "So what?" Well, for one thing, the bridge of many songs is played in the relative major or minor of the home key. If a song is primarily in A minor, but the bridge is decidedly major sounding, chances are it's something based on A minor's relative major: C. Remember this when you're having trouble learning a section of a great song that doesn't seem to fit the mold of the rest of the song, or when you're doing your own songwriting.

Also, if you're soloing, and you're used to playing in A minor but someone throws a song at you in C major, you can use all the same patterns you already know in A minor to solo in C major. They're basically the same key; they have the same "key signature" (the number or sharps or flats). So now you're able to multiply the keys you can solo in by two, because if you're comfortable soloing in A minor, you could, with hardly any changes at all, be just as good soloing in C major.

And there's one thing that makes all this relative stuff really easy to figure out: The relative minor of any note is only three frets down; the relative major of any note is only three frets up—anywhere on the neck. Learning little landmarks like these helps you map out the guitar like never before.

Chart of Relative Major and Minor Keys

Relative Major	Relative Minor
C	A
D♭ (C♯)	B♭ (A♯)
D	B
E♭	C
E	C♯
F	D
F♯ (G♭)	D♯ (E♭)
G	E
A♭	F
A	F♯
B♭	G
B	G♯

14 THE BLUES AIN'T ALL SAD

Musicians who haven't spent much time playing the blues tend to think the genre is all sad and somber, played primarily in a minor key. They're so wrong. Most blues songs are major or dominant, and are typically more upbeat than plodding and morose. Sure, you're probably familiar with any number of slow blues standards, such as "Red House" and "Five Long Years," but any blues artist worth his mojo knows that an entire set of that type of material will bore the pants off even their most ardent fans.

Leave the minor chords at home next time you make it to the local blues jam. Tell the drummer to pick up the pace on that shuffle or swing while you whip the crowd into a frenzy of excitement reminiscent of an authentic New Orleans Mardi Gras festival. It takes major and well-handled dominant seventh chords to fill that bill. For a couple of useful examples of the partyin' side of blues rhythm playing (and another example of what the blues are *not)*, see tip #56.

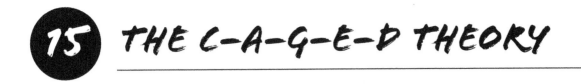

15 THE C-A-G-E-D THEORY

When you're learning guitar, it seems like it will be an eternal process—and it will be, make no mistake about it. But there are some elements of guitar playing that come into better focus with just a few minor adjustments in the way you think of the instrument. For one, a thorough knowledge of chords seems a particularly daunting mountain to climb. One helpful tool on this trek, however, is to realize that there are really only five basic chord shapes. Some methods of teaching touch on this with the "C–A–G–E–D" theory.

The C, A, G, E, and D chord shapes that most of us learn in our first guitar lesson are the five basic chord shapes to which I'm referring. Almost any other chord you'll ever learn is just a souped-up version of your basic open-stringed C, A, G, E, or D chord (or their minor variations), often with just an extra note or two added—even when the fingering seems quite different. Now let's examine a few more colorful chords. Think visually (fretboard shapes) and notice how they all relate back to one of those original five. This visualization exercise should help you more easily categorize the chords you learn. I'll just show a few examples for each of the five basic chords here. You'll discover many more on your own, I'm sure. For more on chords and inversions, see tips #16 and #57.

C chord variations

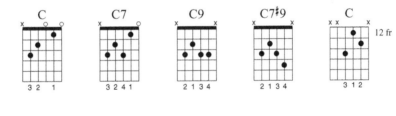

A chord variations

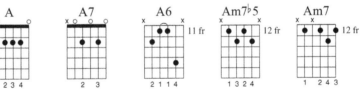

G chord variations

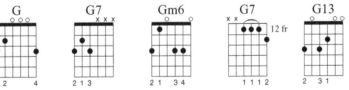

E chord variations

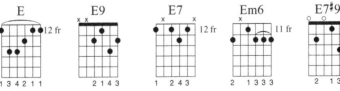

D chord variations

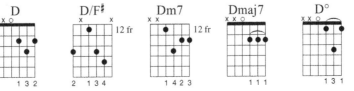

16   THE ABCs AND 123s OF CHORDS

Unless you never leave your house to get out and jam with living, breathing musicians, chances are you're going to spend far more time playing chords and rhythm guitar than you'll ever spend playing lead guitar. And if you're into the acoustic thing, and you prefer to strum and hum by the fireplace at night, you're probably already aware of how integral a working knowledge of chords is to your enjoyment of the guitar. Everybody wants to know more chords.

Either way, it makes sense that you should learn everything you can about chords and their construction. Really, chords are far easier to understand than most people think. If you know your ABC's up to G, and you can count to 13, you've already got the basic info.

Chords are made up of scale tones (yet another reason for you to understand at least the basics of both major and minor scales, even if you're not interested in becoming a shreddin' lead player—see tip #2.)

Major chords

Let's build a major chord on the note C. Here's how it works: Start with the note C, then skip the next note in the C major scale (D). You'll need the third note in the C major scale (E). Then we'll skip the next note (F) and use the fifth note in the scale (G). There's your basic C major chord: C, E, and G. Now play the basic open-position C chord you learned your first week on the guitar and look at what notes you're playing: C at the third fret on the fifth string, E at the second fret on the fourth string, the open G or third string, C at the first fret on the second string, and the open E or first string. All major chords are made up of the notes 1, 3, and 5 from the major scale beginning on the chosen "root" note. Any major chord you analyze on the neck of the guitar will have this same relationship between notes, based on the root note of the chord.

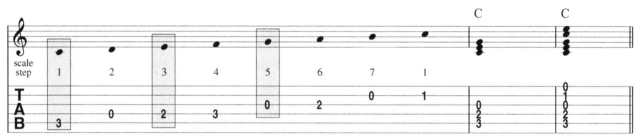

Minor chords

Similarly, all minor chords are built using a 1–3–5 pattern—the 1, $\flat$ or "minor" 3, and 5 of the chosen root note of the minor chord. All minor chords have a ($\flat$) or minor 3rd instead of a "major" 3rd. Look at the basic A minor chord you learned early on, and what notes do you have: the open A or fifth string, E at the second fret on the fourth string, A at the second fret on the third string, C at the first fret on the second string, and the open E or first string.

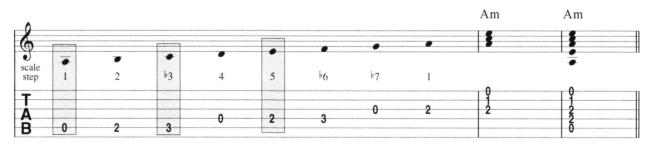

And check this out: Change the ♭3rd of this A minor chord (C at the first fret on the second string) to a "major" 3rd—a C♯ at the second fret on the second string—and you've changed your A minor chord to an A major chord. There is only a one-fret difference between any major and minor chord, anywhere on the neck of the guitar.

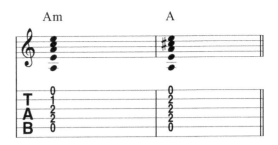

Seventh chords

Now let's take the ABC's and 123's a little further and build some 7th and 9th chords. Expanding on what you've just learned, that a basic major or minor chord is made up of the notes 1, 3, and 5 (major chord) or 1, ♭3, and 5 (minor chord), it should be easy to understand that to make a 7th chord, you just add the 7th note above the root note. And just like there are major and minor 3rds, there are major and minor 7ths. The major 7th of C is B, making a C major 7th chord: C–E–G–B. The minor (or "dominant") 7th of C is B♭, making a C7 or C dominant 7th chord: C–E–G–B♭. Likewise for the minor chord: A minor 7 is "spelled" or made up of A, C, E, and G. (Minor chords with major 7ths are not often used, but an A minor/major 7 is spelled A–C–E–G♯.)

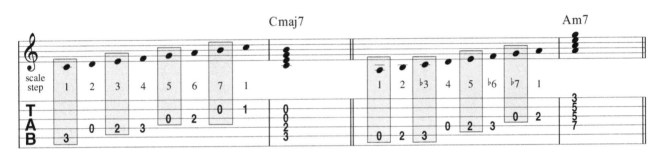

Extended chords

Building chords with even further "extensions" follows the same pattern. Also, the numbering of the scale tones must continue into a second octave to reach the 9th and 13th notes, from which we build more extended chords. Notice that the root note (1), the 3rd, 5th, and 7th are always referred to the same, regardless of octave. The 2nd scale step is referred to as the 9th in the second octave, the 4th step is sometimes referred to as the 11th, and the 6th step is referred to as the 13th in the second octave.

A C9 chord would be spelled C–E–G–B♭–D. An Am9 chord would be spelled A–C–E–G–B. And going beyond that, the next most common chord you might encounter—especially if you're playing funk, jazz, western swing, or blues—is a 13th chord. A 13th chord might be spelled (or numbered) 1–3–5–7–9–11–13. But we don't often use the 11th note in a chord. (Besides, that would make for seven notes, which is more than most guitarists can play at one time.)

In fact, you don't need all the notes that we've spelled out for these extended chords, because some notes can simply be "implied" to make the chord easier to play and actually easier to listen to as well. In many chords you'll encounter, the 5th and root note are left out. The 3rd of the chord (which tells us if the chord is major or minor) and the "flavor" notes (such as the 7th, 9th, 13th, etc.) are always included.

In the example at right, the C13 chord has no 5th (G), and the Am9 chord has no root note (A). These notes are implied. Also note that the C13 chord has a ♭7th (B♭) instead of the B♮ found in a C major scale. Most 9th and 13th chords are built over a "dominant" chord, featuring a ♭7th (or dominant 7th), instead of a major 7th. (For more on scale steps, see tip #2.)

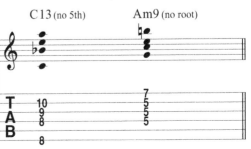

Soloing is an art form that takes most of us years to perfect—if any of us actually do "perfect" soloing. But here's one trick that will instantly "professionalize" your soloing abilities: Base your solos on the arpeggios of the chords you'll be soloing over. If your chord progression goes C–Am–Dm–G–C, focus your playing on at least some of the notes in the C chord (C–E–G) over the C chord, the notes in the Am chord (A–C–E) over the Am chord, the notes in the Dm chord (D–F–A) over the Dm chord, and the notes in the G chord (G–B–D) over the G chord. (See tip #16 for more on building chords.)

Soloing using arpeggio tones

TRACK 13

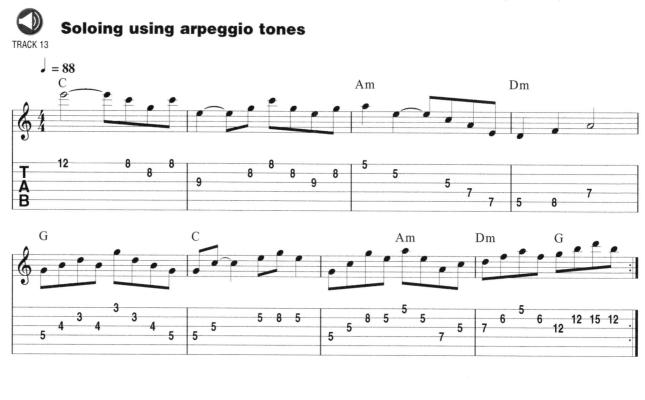

Here's the same progression for you to practice with:

TRACK 14

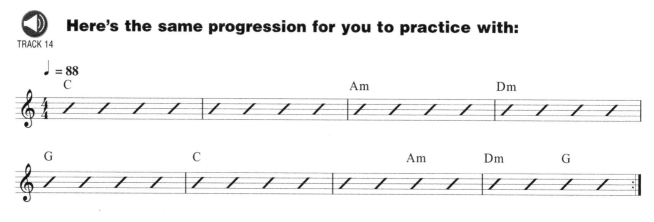

If you're jamming on a I–IV–V blues tune at an open mic night somewhere, say in the key of A, try playing an A arpeggio (A–C#–E) over the A chord, a D arpeggio (D–F#–A) over the D chord, and an E arpeggio (E–G#–B) over the E chord. Once you've mastered that, try playing 7th and 9th chord arpeggios. The A7 arpeggio is A–C#–E–G, the A9 arpeggio is A–C#–E–G–B, the D7 arpeggio is D–F#–A–C, the D9 arpeggio is D–F#–A–C–E, the E7 arpeggio is E–G#–B–D, and the E9 arpeggio is E–G#–B–D–F#.

Using arpeggio lines over a blues in A

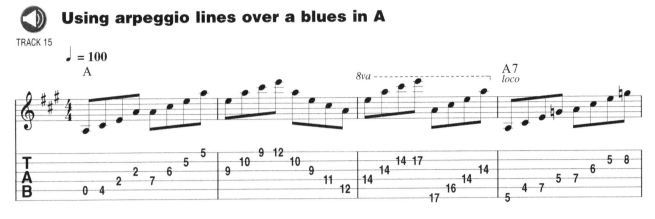

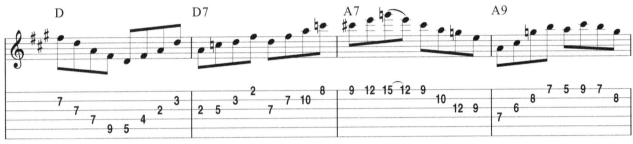

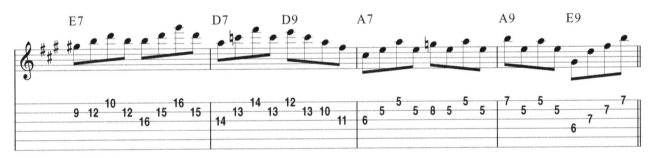

Here's the same progression for you to practice with:

TRACK 16

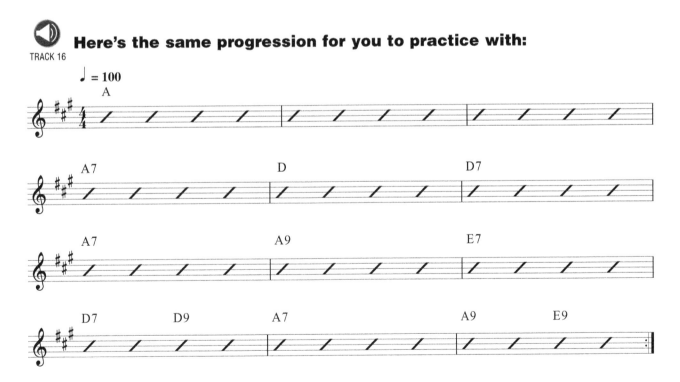

Now this technique might actually sound too simplistic in a real application, but it's simply meant to be used as a guideline to improve your soloing. It's up to you to learn ways to incorporate arpeggios—as well as "passing" or non-chord tones—into your actual lead riffs. But once you do, your solos will instantly make more sense to you and your audience. And when you get really good at it, you'll be able to play almost *a capella*—without any other instruments—and still have the chord structure of the song remain recognizable to your listeners.

23

18 FOUR FINGERS, PLEASE

I can't imagine why anyone would purposely operate at only 75 percent efficiency on their instrument, but that's exactly what you're doing if you play without using your little finger on your fretting hand. If you need some exercises to strengthen your pinky so you can put it to use, see tip #19.

19 WARM-UPS MADE EASY

Whenever my fretting hand starts to stiffen up and slow down—like when I'm just not playing enough—I get back to the ultimate basics of improving my fret-hand dexterity. Scales and riffs are great, but by using this simple warm-up routine you'll get every finger, and every combination of fingers, ripping again, and you'll barely even have to think about it as you're doing it. With each of these exercises, you'll want to play across all six strings, from low to high and back again or from high to low and back again, using just the fingers indicated. Alternate pick each of these drills, and when you think you've mastered them all, try playing them backwards. (For more on alternate picking, including three great alternate picking exercises, see tip #20.)

Warm-up #1

After you've finished at the first and second frets (as shown below), move up one fret and repeat. Continue moving up one fret at a time until you've run out of frets. Then repeat this exact same exercise using just your second and third fingers, and then just your third and fourth fingers. You'll really feel this workout when using your third and fourth fingers.

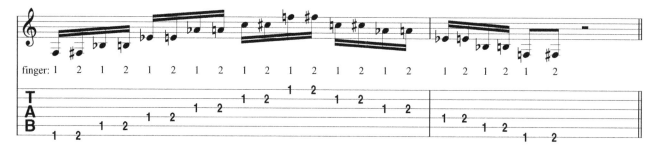

Warm-up #2

After you've finished at the first and third frets (as shown), move up one fret and repeat. Continue moving up one fret at a time until you've run out of frets. Then repeat this exact same exercise using just your second and fourth fingers. Again, you'll really feel this workout any time you're using your fourth finger.

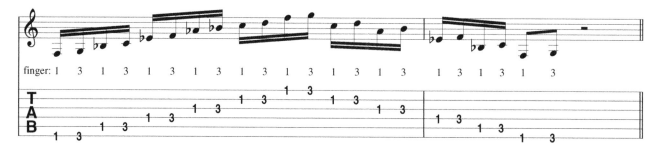

Warm-up #3

Continue this pattern as you did in warm-ups #1 and 2.

Warm-up #4

This one will cause you to stretch a bit. Proceed across the strings and up the neck as before. When you're done with the first and second fingers, use your first and third finger, playing the first and fourth frets (stretching three frets). Then, using your first and fourth finger, stretch out playing the first and fifth frets.

The next three exercises focus on three-finger drills. Warm-up #6 in particular emulates scale fragments, so it really applies almost directly to your soloing skills.

Warm-up #5

This exercise will challenge your alternate picking technique a little, but it's more about your fretting hand. Proceed across the strings and up the neck as before. When you're done with the first, second, and third fingers, use your second, third, and fourth fingers, which will really be tiring for most people—but that's exactly what these warm-ups are for. You'll play so much more precisely after putting your fingers through this workout.

Warm-up #6

Proceed across the strings and up the neck as before. When you're done with the first, second, and fourth fingers, use your first, third, and fourth fingers (playing the first, third, and fourth frets to begin the exercise). Then start over using your first, second, and fourth fingers, stretched a bit.

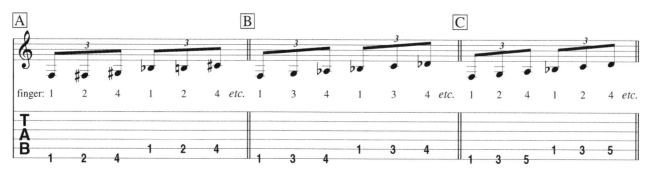

Warm-up #7

Now we'll really stretch out your fretting hand. This is similar to warm-up #6, but with more stretching. It can be quite tough at first, but keep at it, and you'll see your playing improve because of your extra effort. Continue across and up as usual. When you're done with the first, second, and fourth fingers, use your first, third, and fourth fingers.

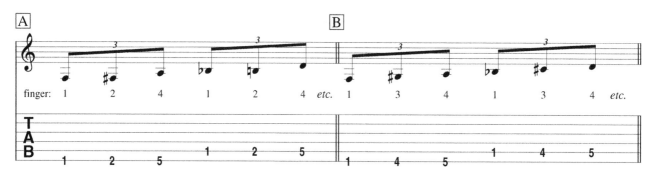

20 ALTERNATE PICKING

If you're not already using alternate picking, you have to start now. Here are a few simple exercises to get your up-and-down skills together:

A simple up-and-down pattern

Using a downstroke, then an upstroke for each fret, lay down all four fingers one-at-a-time in open position, across all six strings and back. Then move up a fret and do it again until you've played the whole neck, or until your hand falls off. Use a metronome and keep your playing clean. If you're playing sloppy, you're playing too fast.

In groups of three

Use a regular scale for this exercise and pay close attention to your picking direction until you get the hang of it. I've written this out in C major. Play the scale across all six strings and back again.

Speed drill in sixteenth-note triplets

I've written this one out in C major, too. Play across all six strings and back. Using a metronome, start extremely slow and speed up only as much as you can handle while still playing *clean*. Clean is the key. Count this figure "one-trip-let, *and*-trip-let; two-trip-let, *and*-trip-let; three-trip-let, *and*-trip-let; four-trip-let, *and*-trip-let."

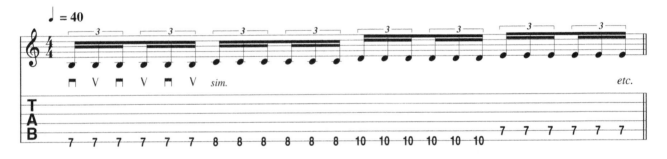

Speed drill in thirty-second notes, groups of four

Again, start extremely slow, and speed up only as much as you can handle while still playing clean. You can count this "one-e-and-a, *and*-e-and-a; two-e-and-a, *and*-e-and-a; three-e-and-a, *and*-e-and-a; four-e-and-a, *and*-e-and-a."

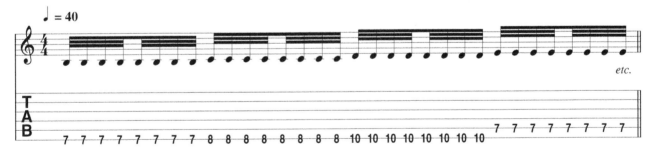

21 GETTA TUNA

When was the last time you saw a pro musician offend the audience's ears attempting to tune up by playing two out-of-sync strings and turning the tuning pegs? It doesn't happen. Pros use electronic tuners, and often have them "in-line"—meaning that they're plugged into the tuner at all times, and the tuner is between their guitar and their amp in the circuit. And in many cases, a pro musician will also have a volume pedal arranged so that they can turn off the sound coming through their amplifier speakers while tuning using their electronic tuner (which usually require that the guitar's—not the amp's—volume be turned up). If they don't handle it that way, they'll usually flick the amp's standby switch to turn off the speakers while they tune up.

Besides, you'll be happier with your own playing and feel like you're learning and advancing faster if you're always in tune—which you should be once you have an electronic tuner. Many electronic tuners work without even plugging into them, so you can tune an acoustic guitar using an electric tuner just by setting the tuner near your guitar and playing an open string. And if you ever decide to do your own guitar intonation (see tip #87), a good electronic tuner will make the job so much easier.

So do yourself—and everyone listening to you—a favor, and get a tuner. They go for as little as $20 these days, and they're well worth it. I use a Boss TU-12H, which worked just fine when I teched for Sammy Hagar and his entire band (the TU-12H even tunes bass guitars). It's probably the most popular tuner out there; most guitar techs I talk to seem to use one. It's a little more expensive, but worth every penny.

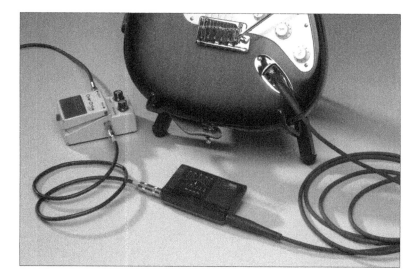

 22 SOUNDHOLE SOLUTION

We've all spent ridiculous amounts of time shaking our acoustic guitars, attempting to recover a pick we've dropped into the soundhole. It has often seemed inconceivable to me that I couldn't quickly shake some-

thing out of my acoustic, but I can't recall ever having pulled it off without having almost totally ruined the mood for playing. Here's the easy way around the problem: Hold the guitar flat, with the strings and soundhole facing the ceiling. Shake the guitar gently until the lost item appears directly under the soundhole opening. Using a pencil, pin the item to the inside back of the guitar (use the eraser side). Carefully turn the guitar upside down while maintaining a hold on the item with the pencil, then let go and let it fall out of your guitar. Problem solved.

 23 ELECTRIC VS. ACOUSTIC, PT. 1

It always cracks me up when someone, who I've just told that I play guitar, asks if I play electric or acoustic guitar. If they had asked, "Which do you play more often, electric or acoustic?"—now that would be a valid question. But the answer to the more common question has to be: "Both, of course, you moron." OK, you can leave the insult out and just say, "Both, of course."

Because if you play one, you play both—even if you've never tried yet. They're the exact same instrument. Go into any music store, where all the guitars, electric and acoustic, are sure to be tuned to standard A-440 tuning, and you'll be able to play the same chords and the same notes and the same songs on either electric or acoustic guitar. It might be easier to play some things on an electric guitar than on an acoustic guitar, especially higher on the neck. But understand: They're the exact same instrument. One is just made to be more easily amplified, that's all. If you've had any hesitation about cross-hitting on acoustic or electric, don't. Step up to the plate and swing for the fences.

 24 ELECTRIC VS. ACOUSTIC, PT. 2

OK, they're the same instrument. But they are different animals. Of this, there's no doubt. Things that can easily be done on an electric guitar might not be possible on an acoustic (I've yet to see anyone do a tremolo arm dive bomb on an acoustic guitar). And some things you play may sound better on an acoustic guitar than on an electric guitar—like a gentle fingerpicking-style version of the Beatles "Yesterday," for example. Give both types of guitar a shot, and seek out and explore the differences as well as the similarities.

HEAVIER STRINGS, BETTER TONE

Stevie Ray Vaughan knew it, and so have countless other guitar heroes. The heavier your strings, the better tone you'll hear from them. This has to do with both physics and magnetic principles, which we really don't need to get into here. But putting a set of strings on your guitar with a high string measuring .010 or .011 will give you a richer, more commanding presence than a set of light gauge strings starting with an .008 high string. The same applies to your lower strings as well. Put a low E (sixth string) measuring .052 on your guitar, and feel the power! Get away from the light gauge and extra-light gauge strings and put a set of medium gauge strings on your guitar, and you'll have a completely changed tone. You might even be happier with your amp and rig because of it. Of course, there's a price to pay for using heavier strings: They're hell on your fingers—at first. You'll get used to them quickly though, if you play often. And you'll break far fewer .011s than .008s or .009s, which is itself almost worth a little pain.

 ## TUBE AMPS SOUND BETTER

They just do. Face it. There's barely a pro touring musician alive who isn't using a tube amplifier in concert. And with the full range of "clean to crunch" made available in tube variations by all the great amp manufacturers, there is no excuse for not having a great-sounding amp—whether it's a small wattage practice amp or a stadium-rocking monster. Solid-state and hybrid amps that don't rely on tubes for the power side of the amplification process (as opposed to the pre-amp side, which supplies much of the tone) are thin and artificial sounding compared to a good tube-driven Fender, Marshall, MESA/Boogie, or whatever your brand preference. Can the canned sound. Go tubular.

 ## AMP MODELERS

While tube amps sound better—particularly live—there's no denying that amp modelers can be *very* convenient. Especially if you're heading into the studio and might need a variety of tones and classic amp sounds. If you're just laying down tracks, there's no need to lug around something big and heavy (or fragile and expensive). In the digital age, more and more top pros are relying on amp modelers in the recording studio, instead of their live rigs. The ease of use and the variety of sounds put right at your fingertips by modelers make up for any perceived deficiencies of tone—which are admittedly becoming more and more difficult to hear, as technology advances.

28 SMALL AMPS, BIG SOUNDS

Music history is jeweled with stories of how classic albums were recorded using the smallest of the small practice amps. To the listening audience, including the millions who bought those albums, the end result sounds nothing short of incredible. You don't need kilowatts of power in a recording studio to make your tracks sound huge. A 10-watt amp the size of a boom-box, cranked up all the way (if you find yourself saying, "This amp goes to 11," then put it there), will sound every bit as good, if not better, than an under-cranked concert-size amp. And it will be much easier for your ears to take, hour after hour in the studio.

That's another very important consideration, too. If your typical rehearsal is three hours, and you leave with your ears buzzing (which is a sign of damage), imagine how worn out they'll be after you've spent an entire day in a recording studio, laying down track after track for your big debut. And if you've spent a bunch of your hard-earned cash to block out 12 hours in a studio, you're going to want to be operating at peak efficiency the entire time, or your recording will suffer and your money will have been wasted.

29 AMP UP, GUITAR DOWN

Novices tend to put their guitar volume all the way up the day they buy the instrument, then leave it there forever. Professionals use their guitar's volume knob incessantly, to control not only their volume, but their tone as well. Even with an overdriven amp, you can usually get clean sound (if you need it, such as when you want to emulate an acoustic guitar intro) simply by turning your guitar volume down. And conversely, if you set your guitar volume about 75 percent of the way up for your crunchy rhythms, you'll have headroom—and increased sustain and bite—for your solos, simply by turning the guitar volume up to 10, even if your amp is set clean. Then set your amp volume a little higher than you did when you kept your guitar volume on 10, and you'll find your tone. Get used to playing rhythm with the guitar volume at about 7, and let the amp do its job.

When sound checking for a live performance, set your guitar volume at about 7, and make your amp as loud as it needs to be to play rhythm guitar. When the front of house sound tech asks you to play something so he or she can set the PA levels, just play rhythm guitar with your amp and guitar set this way. Don't turn your guitar up all the way and start ripping off solos, because he'll then just turn you down in the PA—or more likely will ask you to turn your amp down. Save yourself that extra volume for when the band is cranking full out and you need a little extra punch to cut through the clutter. Sometimes you have to be a little tricky, hiding a little extra volume on your guitar from the sound tech, in order to feel like you're getting the right tone during the show.

30 GIG BAGS VS. SHELLS

Gig bags with over-the-shoulder carrying straps are a blessing. If you've never tried one, once you do you'll kick yourself for not getting one sooner. They're so much easier to deal with than traditional hard-shell guitar cases, and because you'll be wearing your guitar over your shoulder on your way into and out of the venue or studio, you'll be pretty unlikely to bash the guitar against anything that will cause damage. So any worries that the soft gig bag won't protect your guitar from dings flies out the window right there. Besides, because it's so easy to carry your guitar in a gig bag, you'll be likely to keep it closer to you than you would if you were instead lugging a hard shell case around, which will make it less likely that your axe will be stolen. Shells belong on the beach; get a gig bag.

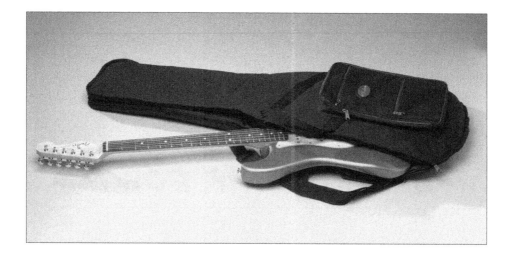

31 CABLE QUALITY

We've come a long way from those old curly cords guitarists plugged in with in the sixties. Those thin, often unshielded cables literally filtered out part of the sound that we all prize quality or vintage guitars for today, particularly in the high end. Don't skimp on your cords. You probably only need one or two long cords anyway. (To connect pedals, you should use the little 6-inch connector cords available everywhere, if only because it cleans up your pedal board).

Well-built cords typically last for years, so dig deep for some spare change and get the high-quality stuff next time you need a new one. Compared to the outlay for your guitar and amp, even the most expensive cords cost next to nothing, so go ahead and splurge. Your tone will improve—at least a little bit, and perhaps dramatically. Plus, the better cords can take more punishment and are usually guaranteed for life by the manufacturer (so save the receipt and/or packaging).

Also, if you get a cord with a "shorted" jack—meaning the cord actually shorts out (on purpose) when you pull it out of your guitar—you won't have to wince anymore as your amplifier suddenly pops and begins to buzz, the way it does with most guitar cords. Shorted jacks go for around $15 a pop (I hate pops, don't you?), but attached to a quality cable, they're well worth the extra expense.

32 GAIN AND SUSTAIN

Most electric guitarists spend their lives searching for the ultimate tone. And always near the top of the list of desires is increased sustain and often a little more drive or "bite." The most common fix thrown at these problems is a distortion pedal. But distortion, in many cases, is not the answer. Sure, a certain amount of "distortion" is what electric guitar is really all about, but you wouldn't listen to a favorite CD if it was buried under distortion.

Treat your guitar signal the same, adding distortion only when you really want distortion, which is defined by electronics or sound engineers as a harsh, clipped sound. If you're using a distortion pedal to get more sustain and drive and aren't happy with the results—particularly for your rhythm guitar tone—turn off or unplug the pedal, then do everything you can to boost the gain of your signal without the distortion pedal.

Gain, in very simple terms, refers to the strength of the signal. The more gain you add to your signal, the more sustain and overdrive—a smoother, less clipped form of distortion—you'll send to your speakers. Many amp designs include two volume controls: a master volume and another knob that is often simply labeled "volume." Set your master volume lower and turn up the other volume knob. This increases the gain of your amplifier's pre-amp section, which boosts the signal coming from the guitar to a level where your amplifier's big power tubes (controlled by the master volume) can turn it into serious volume. With the pre-amp set too low, you're asking the power section of your amp to boost a weak signal. The result is poor tone and, sometimes, increased noise. Also, adjusting your guitar's volume knob comes into play here as well, as suggested in tip #29.

If you're still not hearing the tone you want after boosting your pre-amp volume (and gain), or if your amp only has one volume knob, you can use an overdrive, distortion, or compressor pedal—with the level (volume) set high but the drive (effect) set low—to drive your amp harder, creating more gain and sustain. Many major stars have used this technique to get the tone they wanted, including most notably Stevie Ray Vaughan, with his Ibanez TS-9 Tube Screamer.

The audio track allows you to hear heavy distortion vs. a cleaner, but still crunchy, gain-driven overdrive.

TRACK 17

33 HEAR THE RIG

Jimi Hendrix did not play a Les Paul. Jimi used a Strat through a Cry Baby. That's largely why Jimi sounds like Jimi. And that's why he sounds totally (tonally speaking) different than B.B. King, who uses a semi-hollowbody guitar; and from Jimmy Page, who primarily used a Les Paul; and from T-Bone Walker, who used a big hollowbody jazz guitar. Study this stuff and learn to hear the sound of the setup. What guitar is it? What kind of amp? What effects are being used in the verse, but not during the chorus? Research guitar, amp, and effect sounds in a music store, if you don't have all the requisite toys spread out in your rehearsal room, and then quiz yourself against the radio on a regular basis. It will help you down the road when you're recording your own music and you realize that laying down the same sounds on every single track just might sound boring. At that point, you'll be able to spice up your recordings with a full palette of aural fixations, drawn from your broad, historic understanding of guitar/amp/effect tonal possibilities.

34 DISTORTION VS. OVERDRIVE

Both distortion and overdrive pedals "clip" your signal, filtering out the high and low frequencies of the guitar's natural, unaffected tone. A distortion pedal clips more than an overdrive pedal, creating a harsher sound than the more natural, warmer-sounding "crunch" of an overdrive pedal. Players who are looking for a tone that is still driven, but smoother than their distortion pedal can offer, should try any of the numerous overdrive pedals on the market. Players who want an extreme sound should seek out their favorite distortion pedal.

35 CLEAN AND COMPRESSED

When the gain on your amp or the distortion of your pedals just ain't working for the tune you're playing, but your amp's clean setting is just too dry, try punching it up with a compressor. Besides balancing the overall tone of your guitar, compression has the tendency to add a bit of sustain as well. Sometimes this is just the answer, especially for certain rhythm parts where distortion is just too distorted, and clean is just too, uh, clean.

36 YOUR HEROES ALL CHEAT

You're never going to duplicate their tone. *They're* never going to duplicate their tone—not live anyways. Since at least the mid-sixties, rock stars have been multi-tracking their rhythm parts, laying down two, three, and sometimes more rhythm guitar parts on each song to get a bigger sound. Add to that the fact that they may record each of these different tracks with different guitars, amps, and effects settings, and no one person will ever be able to duplicate that exact sound ever again—not even the artist him- or herself. So stop agonizing over this. Do a little research into what gear that artist used in the studio, what they use live, and then just do your best to replicate what sounds good to you using the equipment you have or can afford to add to your collection.

37 PEDAL POSITIONING

Yes, there is a correct order for your stomp boxes and foot pedals. Connecting your effects pedals in the wrong order can decrease their effectiveness or accuracy and muddy your sound. Follow these general guidelines for pedal placement:

- If you use an octave pedal, it should come at the beginning of your signal chain, right after the guitar. Putting the octave pedal after a chorus, delay, wah-wah, reverb, distortion, or overdrive pedal could negatively affect the octave pedal's pitch accuracy.

- Compressors and limiters should go *before* everything except octave pedals.

- Distortion and overdrive pedals should go *after* octave pedals and compressor/limiters, but *before* equalizers, modulators, volume pedals, delays, chorus, reverb, or tremolo.

- Place equalizers *after* distortion and overdrive pedals.

- Place a volume pedal *before* your delay effects so as not to cut off the delay and reverberation when lowering the volume.

- Put modulators, delay, chorus, wah-wah, reverb, or tremolo pedals toward the end of your signal chain. Reverb or tremolo should come last, right before your amp.

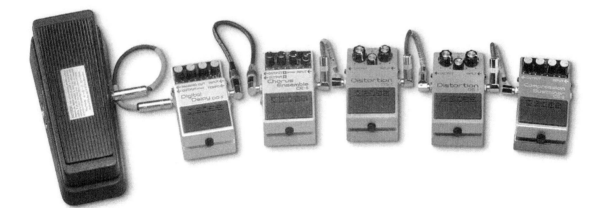

Accidentally pulling your guitar cable out of your floor effects pedals mid-solo comes right after pulling your cord out of your guitar on the bummer-scale. And sometimes it's even worse, because a cable can look like it's fully plugged into a stomp box when it's not, sending you frantically searching in other directions looking for the problem, while your bandmates glare at you unkindly and your audience loses interest.

Don't be afraid to use a little duct tape to secure your cord to your pedals, or to the floor right next to the pedal. You'll probably only need to worry about the cord leading into the first pedal in the chain. This is the connection most susceptible to coming undone, especially if you regularly run to the far end of the stage while hamming it up for the crowd.

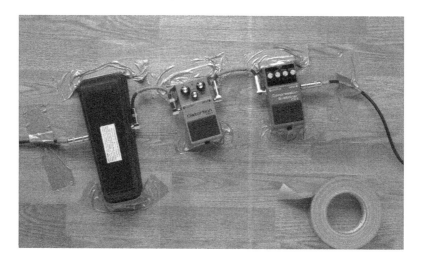

39 *PEDAL BOARDS*

It's a major hassle to have to plug in and unplug all your effects pedals before and after every rehearsal, show, or studio session. Plus it adds a lot of wear and tear on your gear. There's a solution: Buy or build a pedal board, just like the pros use. It will keep your pedals in order, speed your set up and tear down, and—if you get one with a built-in AC adapter—can end forever your addiction to expensive batteries. If you use more than one or two battery operated devices and play regularly, the savings in batteries alone could soon cover the cost of the pedal board.

Any music store can order a high-quality effects pedal floor case for you if they don't already have one in stock. In addition, there are many builders to be found on the Internet who will set you up with a custom-built board made specifically to hold and power your pedals, in exactly the order you want them.

If you'd prefer to build your own, follow these steps:

- Set up your pedals, with cables attached, exactly as you normally would.
- Measure a rectangle around the pedals with a tape measure. Allow some extra space for future additions.
- Cut a 3/4 inch piece of plywood to those measurements.
- Glue a piece of ozite, indoor-outdoor, or berber carpeting to the plywood.
- Attach a couple of kitchen drawer-style handles to the top on each end.

- Attach your pedals to the board using Velcro, or better yet, 3M Dual Lock.
- Cable up.

Note that many battery-operated pedals cannot be left plugged in without draining the batteries. Unless you're using AC adapters with your pedals, you may have to partially unplug them when you're not using them.

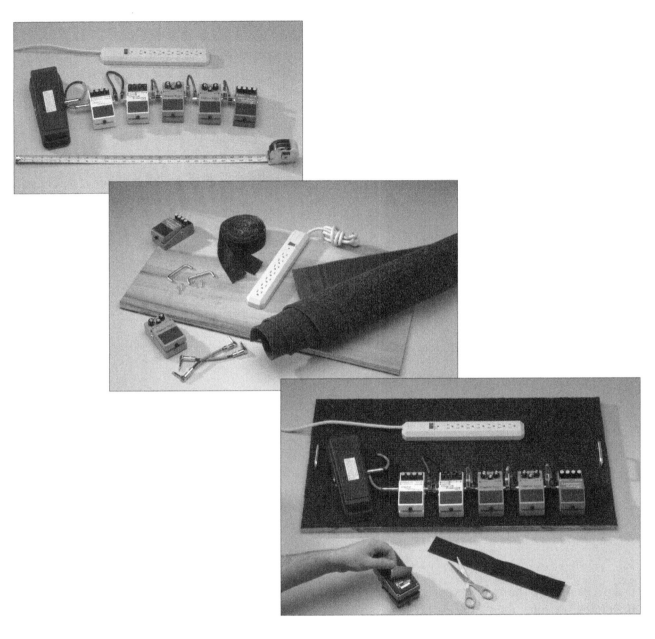

40 CARRY THAT WEIGHT

Wider is better, especially if you're going to "rock and roll all night." A wider strap spreads the weight of your guitar out over a broader area on your shoulder, easing the strain, fatigue, and tension that will eventually build up if you've got a long night ahead of you. And realize that strain and fatigue will work its way right down your arm from your shoulder to your fingers, impacting your playing in a not-so-positive way. Guitar straps allow us to make a bit of a fashion statement, it's true, but the best strap is one you won't notice after a couple of hours of playing. Go wide.

 41 KEEP YOUR STRAP ON

Not only is it embarrassing when your guitar strap unexpectedly gives way, you truly do look foolish and unprofessional when it happens. If you're going to be playing live regularly, standing up, put a set of Strap-loks on your guitar to keep your axe right where it's supposed to be. If you're going to be jumping all over the stage like your pants are on fire, you should consider using a few feet of duct tape to secure your strap even more effectively to the guitar. However, do this knowing the tape can potentially damage the finish on your guitar.

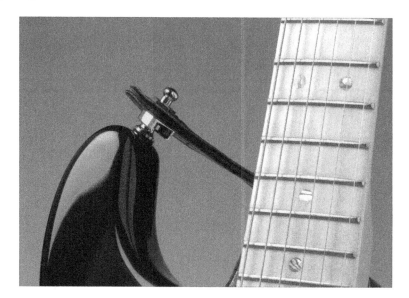

 42 LOOP IT OR LOSE IT

There's little in life more aggravating than taking off on a solo in front of a screaming throng of your most hardcore fans, then stepping on your cable and unplugging your guitar. Usually, by the time you reconnect, your lead break is over. Tough luck, Charlie. If you haven't already figured it out, you need to loop your cord once around your guitar strap to prevent this sort of "premature de-jack-ulation."

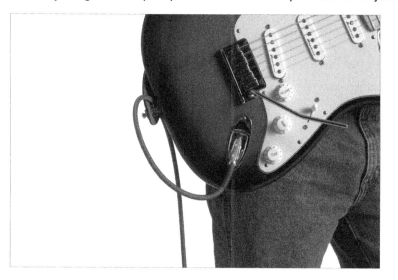

 43 DON'T TURN UP, TILT UP

If you're playing through a combo amp and can't hear yourself, don't turn the volume up if you can tilt the amp up. The same goes for speaker cabinets. Just a few degrees of upward angle will make all the difference in the world in how well you can hear yourself play. There are few audiences you'll ever play for when someone won't complain that you're too loud. But you'll probably never feel that way yourself; you'll always feel like you play better when it's a little louder.

Guitar amplifiers and speaker cabinets are extremely directional beasts, and placing your ears just slightly out of the "spray" of those speaker cones decreases the apparent volume tremendously. A little bit of upward angle will work wonders for giving you all the volume you need, while sparing your audience from a few more needless decibels. What can you use if your amp doesn't have tilt legs? Try a power strip (turn it on its side if you need to plug into it), a rack case cover, a broken distortion pedal, a phone book, a cymbal stand (ask your drummer first), a stack of your unsold debut CDs (hey, you've got to get your money's worth out of them, right?), or just lean your amp against a wall. Just remember: Don't turn up, tilt up.

 **HEAVY PICKS**

Thin guitar picks (plectrums) are fine if you're playing quietly late at night, so as not to wake your prima-donna singer while the tour bus rolls down the road. But besides inhibiting your volume, they also rob you of tone and control. Stiffer picks—particularly those made of materials such as Tortex, or even metal, stone, or bone—really set your strings vibrating in a way that a thin, overly flexible piece of celluloid never will. Two solid objects striking each other will always resonate more effectively than will two soft objects. Think of thin picks as the soft objects, something to be avoided—or weened off of if you currently think you can't live without them.

And with the better tone of a thicker pick or a pick made of a stiffer material comes increased control, especially for lead guitar playing or rapid single-note playing. Think of it this way: You wouldn't score many points playing ping-pong with a flexible paddle. It's the same concept with guitar picks—a thin or celluloid pick is too busy flexing to keep up with your demand for precision playing at high speed. Thicken up.

 PRACTICE FOR PERFECTION

Steve Vai told me that he practices his songs and solos until he can play them twenty-one times in a row, at tempo, without one single mistake. One blunder—even the slightest error in bending or vibrato—and Steve starts the whole cycle of twenty-one over again. Now I'm not saying you should torture yourself trying to live up to Steve Vai's demanding practice regimen, but there are definitely a couple of lessons to be learned here.

First, you can't expect to play anything perfectly if you haven't practiced it perfectly, which Steve obviously does. If you leave the mistakes in while you're practicing, they'll always be ready to jump up and ruin a performance. Use a metronome, drum machine, or other rhythm device to keep time and to mark your progress (see tip #59).

Start out slow—painfully slow, if necessary—and increase the tempo only after you've thoroughly mastered the riff or chord change, meaning that you can play it repeatedly without a screw up, not just one or two lucky times through. If you start to feel a little burned out playing something over and over, alternate the exercise with something less frustrating, putting your nose back to the grindstone as soon as you feel relaxed and up to the challenge again. Use a little of that competitive spirit that resides in all of us to live up to that challenge.

And second, if you're fortunate enough to be as successful as Steve Vai, you'll be playing your songs live in concert hundreds if not thousands of times throughout your career, so running through them a few dozen times in advance is really no big deal. In fact, consider that you may never have the success you're looking for if you don't perfect your material first.

46 GUITAR TV

Many people, myself included, seem to lose their focus after approximately sixty to ninety minutes of continuous guitar playing. But I learned long ago that I can play guitar all the way through a three-hour football game, and easily through a two-hour movie, using the TV to keep my mind satisfied while my fingers did their very necessary equivalent to an athlete's calisthenics or weight training regimen. No, you won't be paying strict attention to a song or scale or whatever, but if you just set up a routine of scales and exercises mixed with a few particularly difficult riffs you're just trying to burn into your muscle memory, you'll benefit greatly from this endeavor. There's nothing better for your speed and dexterity on a Tuesday night rehearsal than a Monday Night Football game spent running your fingers up and down the fretboard. Give it a try.

47 VIDEO TEACHERS

Some of the best instructional videos go for $50 a shot. But they're almost always worth it, especially if it will help you to understand the methods of your favorite guitarist. Video is simply the best way to learn, better in most cases even than private lessons. You can't rewind a private instructor 400 times until you get the lick just right. And you can't count on a private instructor being there for you 24/7/365. There are hundreds, probably thousands, of incredible instructional videos, CD-ROMs, and DVDs available today, covering every style of guitar playing imaginable, from the most hoedownest honky-tonk, to the most jammin' jazz, to the most rip-snortin' rock. No matter your current playing level, there is a 60-minute video lesson out there that will take you weeks, possibly months, to fully absorb, challenging you every fret of the way. Go ahead, rewind it 401 times.

48 NETWORK NEWS

You never know what opportunity will come of a chance meeting. And don't go judgin' no books by their covers either—just because you're not interested in a funk gig doesn't mean the guy that offered it to you doesn't know a mean heavy metal band that needs a new guitarist, too. If you can't carry on simple, friendly conversations with musicians of all types, you'll never know what coveted opportunity may have just passed you by.

And here's another key to career success: Don't badmouth a working musician for "selling out." Go ahead; try it: Quit your slave-wages day job in the warehouse and see how much food you put in your tattoo covered-stomach playing your totally bad-ass all-original conglomeration of polka and trip-hop/metal. Then cut a fellow musician some slack. When you grow up and earn enough cash playing guitar to pay your mortgage, your car payment, your insurance bills, and still have enough left over to stuff your face with Big Macs three times a day, then you're welcome to trash the guy who plays guitar for John Tesh (whom I happened to teach and now makes far more money traveling the world playing guitar than either you or I may ever see).

49 OTHER INSTRUMENTS

We've all got our favorite guitarists, but chances are your favorite guitarists also have favorite saxophone players, or favorite pianists, or favorite symphonic composers as well. There's no doubt about it: Broad listening habits create broad musical imaginations. Not only can you pick up ideas by listening to other genres of music, but you can learn much by listening carefully to instrumentalists playing instruments other than guitar.

The more developed your guitar talents become, the more you will comprehend the licks played by a boogie piano player, bebop sax player, or the first chair violinist in a major symphony orchestra. And the more you listen, the easier it will be for you to simultaneously transfer their licks, mentally, to the guitar fretboard. Because those instruments are physically different than guitars, they allow for combinations of notes or lyrical lines that a guitarist could do, but wouldn't normally think of. Set your ears free, and your imagination will reward you tenfold.

50 ANALYZE YOUR ORIGINALS

If you're into songwriting, analyze your original material in terms of groove and style. And mix it up. Try different tempos, different feels. Unless you're using a musical gimmick to hook your audience—like you're trying to outpace Slayer by playing all your rhythms in sixty-fourth notes at 220 bpm (beats per minute)—you'll just bore the hell out of your listeners (and eventually yourself, too) if you don't cover a range of tempos, grooves, and styles in your songwriting.

For example, if you're writing and playing blues, your set could include slow blues, jazz blues, rock blues, a gospel-tinged tune, funk blues, a Bo Diddley -style tune, a Chuck Berry -style stomper, a Cajun tune, country blues, Delta style bottleneck playing, big band swing, a rhumba blues, and probably more—and still be considered blues by your audience. If you're writing straight-ahead, mainstream rock tunes, you can get away with quoting influences from the Beatles to Mozart to Japanese koto playing and back to Metallica and still be considered a rock band. You get the picture.

Analyze your compositions, your entire repertoire of original tunes, and see where you rate on the "same old, same old" scale. Does everything you write sound and feel the same? Is everything played at the same tempo; does everything share the same dynamics? (Probably always at full volume, right?) Try drawing outside the lines once in awhile by emulating a type of song or groove that you haven't done before. The exercise may not be successful the first time around, but you will grow from the experience, and your creative juices will begin rushing and flooding the more you expand your horizons. And even if the only result is that you start to write better songs in your same old style—which you most likely will—you've still won.

51 SINGING AND PLAYING

Like anything else in music, singing and playing is a skill that takes practice. But that's all it takes—it's certainly not impossible. If you feel your musical career is being hijacked by difficult vocalists, or if you just think it would be fun to sing and play, the time for you to start working on your own vocal skills is now. And no, you don't have to give up guitar playing to become frontman, unless you secretly want to become the next Steven Tyler and are willing to leave the axe-slinging to someone else. Besides, being able to sing at least a halfway decent shout background vocal makes you more valuable to almost any band you'll ever consider joining.

If you have a hard time playing and singing simultaneously, step back a little in your choice of material and get comfortable at the simplest level. Strum and sing old-time folk, blues, children's, or Christmas songs if you must—anything that gets you going—until you build your confidence and coordination. Sing nonsense lyrics if you have to (a lot of successful songwriters lay down their initial ideas that way anyway). Or just hit a chord and simultaneously shout, "Hey!" if that's what it takes to get the ball rolling.

Start crooning over just one chord/strum per measure, gradually adding a few extra up and down sweeps with your pick. Then try singing while you play simple riff-based songs. The next step is to put together a repertoire of material that approaches your long-term goals. You'll eventually be able to work your way back to the music you really want to play or write, no matter how complicated that music may be, and you'll actually enjoy yourself even more than ever before.

Singing and playing can be difficult at first, there's no denying that. But millions of people do it, and you can too. Get started now.

52 SIMPLIFY FOR SONGWRITING

Most successful songwriters can at least strum simple chords and sing at the same time—even if they're not great vocalists and their main function in the band is lead guitarist. From the hundreds of artist interviews I've done, I've learned that's where a great number of hit songs come from: low-key sessions with an acoustic guitar. And typically the artist is playing in a far simpler style when they're writing songs than their fans might expect.

So simplify things when you're writing. If you're primarily an electric player, try writing on acoustic, which will almost automatically force you to play just the basics. You can add the fancy riffs and intricate intros after you've perfected the basic progression/melody of the song and have shown it to the rest of your band. Remember, without great songs, your great solos don't have much of a chance of being heard by the masses.

53 KEEP IT FUN

No matter how hard you push yourself to become a better guitarist, and regardless of how exhaustingly you work at launching a paying musical career for yourself, remember that you first wanted to play guitar because it looked like fun. Back off from the hard work once in awhile and just play something easy, different, or even goofy. Playing guitar is fun. Keep it fun.

Turnarounds are useful far beyond the blues, with which they're most often associated. This stems largely from the fact that so much of rock 'n' roll is blues-based. But there are also jazz turnarounds, country turnarounds, and just plain useful-all-over-the-place turnarounds. Whether you use them to spice up your rhythms or your solos, a few cool turnarounds will turn heads. Try these samples for starters—they're just meant to fuel your imagination—then seek out more on your own. There are books and books full of 'em out there. Turnarounds are infinite—and infinitely useful. For more on turnarounds, see tips #9 and #10.

Classic blues turnarounds
TRACK 18

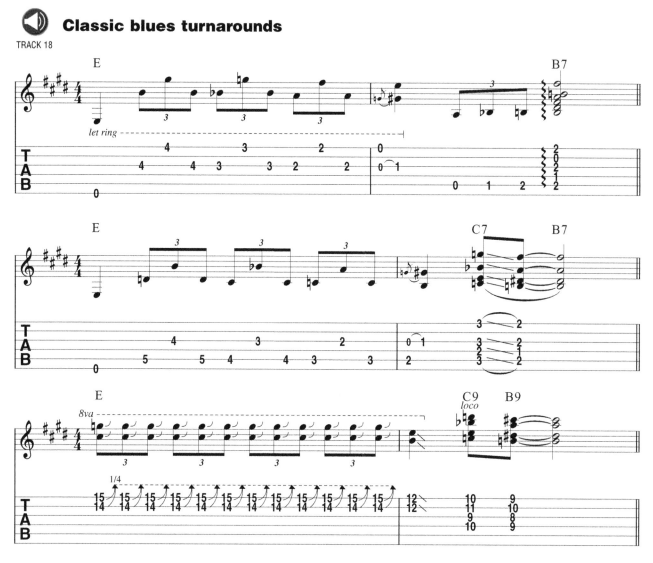

Jazz-swing turnarounds
TRACK 19

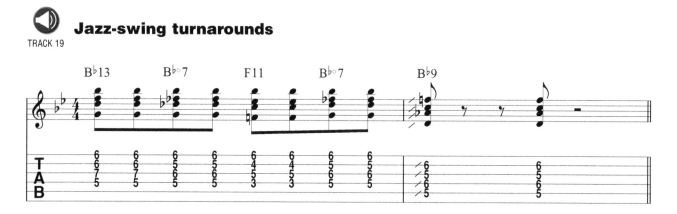

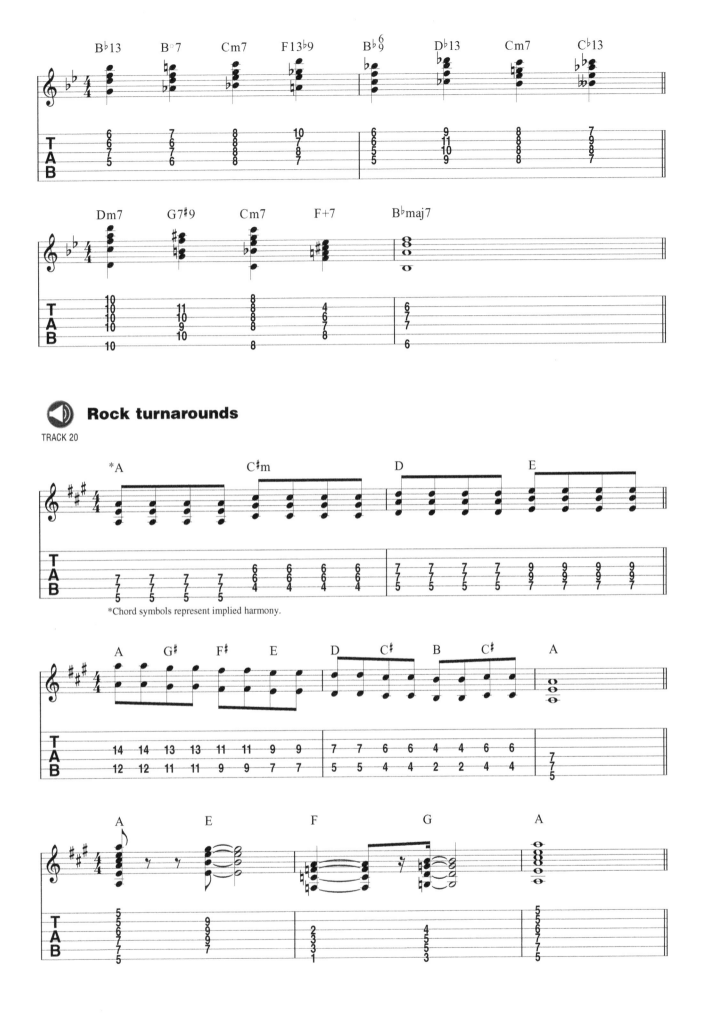

Rock turnarounds

TRACK 20

*Chord symbols represent implied harmony.

Country turnarounds

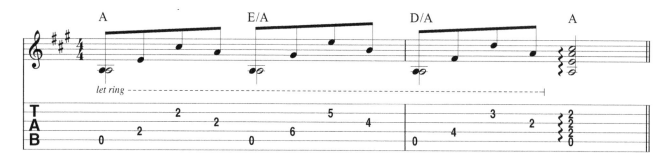

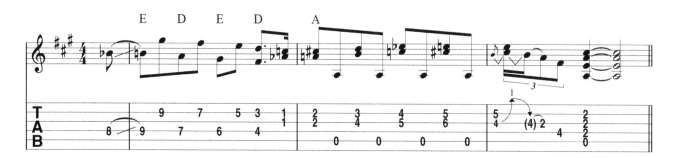

55 EASY FUNK GUITAR

Funk guitar, whether it's the classic dance thang or the souped-up, metallic funk-rock version, allows you to take off on some of the most driving grooves you'll ever play. It's really a fun genre, and its basic moves are far simpler than many players might imagine. Armed with a basic blues scale, a full palette of 9th chords, and maybe a wah pedal, you'll have almost all you'll need to really get your groove on.

Funk guitar parts—the chordal sections that is, as opposed to the heavy blues scale-based riffs so common in funk songs—stick largely to the top four strings of the instrument. Track 22 will enlighten you to five simple 9th chord inversions that perform together as an arpeggiated chord scale. These chords will provide you with endless funk jam possibilities and can be used over the I, IV, and V chords in many funk songs. Track 23 shows the minor versions of these five inversions. So loosen up your wrist and throw your best syncopated, sixteenth-note strumming patterns at these chords:

Five dominant 9th chord inversions

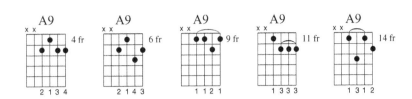

Five minor 9th chord inversions

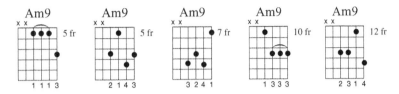

Funk inversion rhythm exercises

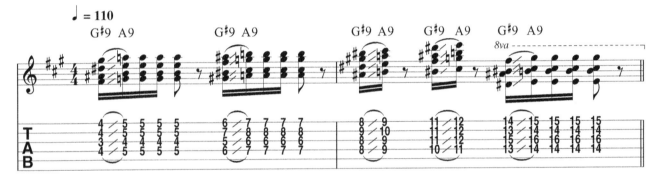

Here is a funk groove in A for you to practice with. You can play either the dominant 9th or the minor 9th chords over this jam track.

56 THIS IS NOT THE BLUES

When most guitarists are faced with a blues tune, they automatically whip out their basic E- and A-position barre chords and then add the 6th and ♭7th with their little fingers. THIS IS NOT THE BLUES. Not really, anyway. That kind of playing might work fine for a Chuck Berry tune or an occasional blues-rock tune, but you're going to have real blues players rolling their eyes if you can't comp with something more authentic. And there is actually something even easier to play—if you can imagine—that will earn your rhythm playing a big thumbs-up from even the most seasoned blues veterans. Learn this simple lick, and a couple variations shown below, then use it on the I, the IV, and the V chord in almost any blues tune you encounter. You'll immediately sound like you've been playing the blues for years.

 Blues-rock rhythm guitar

TRACK 26

 Blues rhythm guitar

TRACK 27

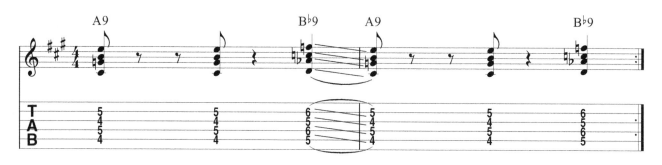

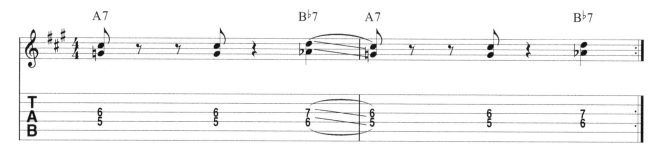

Here is a blues progression in A for you to practice with:

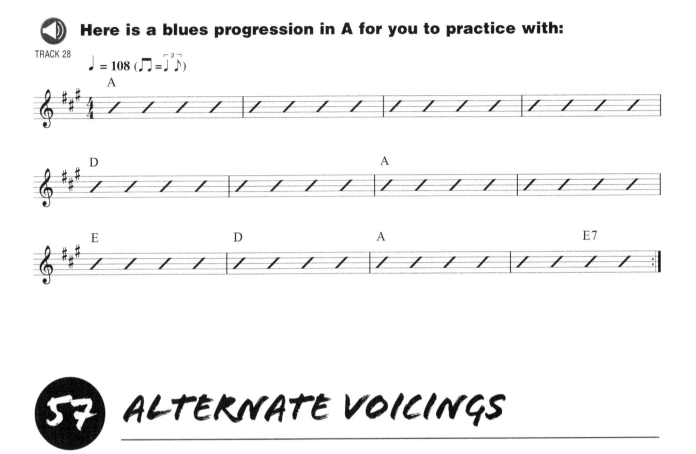

57 ALTERNATE VOICINGS

If you're going to hang on a particular chord for awhile, try mixing up a few different varieties of that same chord to keep yourself and your listening audience from getting bored. For example, if you have a song with an extended section on an E chord, you could just chunk away the whole time with the basic open-position E chord that you learned in your first lesson. But it would be far more interesting, and far more fun too, if you also threw in a few E chords elsewhere on the neck. These substitutes are commonly referred to as inversions or voicings.

Try out the following substitutions over your next long E-chord section and use this concept to add interest to all your chord playing by learning as many chord voicings as you can; there are truckloads of books on the subject available online or at any music store. And remember that you can alternate between strumming, plucking, or arpeggiating the chord to add additional rhythmic interest to your new-found harmonic talents. For more on chords and inversions see tips #15 and #16.

Alternate voicings for an E chord

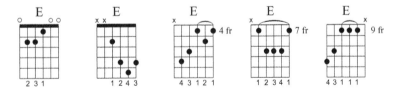

Alternate voicings for an E7 chord

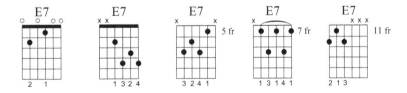

58 DAMP IT

Uncontrolled strings are the enemy. They buzz. They feed back. They muck up our chords and solos with notes that our ears tell us don't belong. There are several methods of controlling these rogue noises, and they're pretty easy to master. Get these two string "damping" techniques together, and your playing will improve noticeably:

Pick-Hand or "Heel" Damping

The most typical and easiest method of damping is to rest the heel of your pick hand on the strings as you strum or pick, slightly—but not completely—deadening the ringing strings. You might even find that, when playing a recurring figure on the low string for example, you might not rest your heel on that string at all, but may have it securely down across the rest of your strings. This is particularly useful when playing rhythm guitar, especially while using a lot of gain or distortion, as a hard rock or heavy metal player might do. The louder you're cranked up and/or the more gain or distortion you're using, the more damping you'll have to use to keep your output musical.

You'll quickly learn how much is too much damping (you can deaden the strings completely by pressing down hard enough) and how much is too little. You'll also want to vary the amount of pressure you put into damping your strings depending on the tone you want to achieve. Typically, you'll use a little more damping during a verse, when the vocalist needs to be front and center, and a little less during the chorus of your song, when you'll often want more volume and attack.

Try this exercise to improve your mastery of pick-hand, heel damping: Play an F barre chord at the first fret. Hold the chord down solidly, then strum the chord using a steady eighth-note pattern. Use all downstrokes for this exercise. Start with no damping and listen to the sound you get. Then, using the pick-hand damping technique described above, lay the heel of your pick hand down on the strings as you strum. Experiment with using more and less heel damping pressure to change the tone and attack of your playing. The more pressure you apply, the more you may want to dig in with the pick; this is another method of changing the tone and attack.

TRACK 29

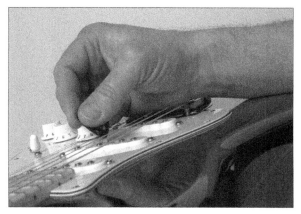

Pick-hand damping

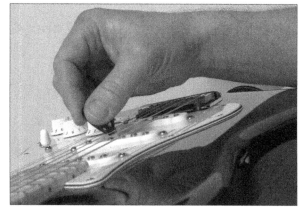

No damping

Fret-Hand Damping

The next most important method of damping involves your fret hand. This technique comes quite naturally to most players, at least after awhile. It primarily involves lifting your fingers just slightly off the fretboard after playing a note or chord, but keeping them in contact with the strings so the strings won't ring. This technique is useful in accenting a rhythmic pattern or in creating a little breathing room in the accompaniment over which a vocalist or soloist can work their magic.

Try this exercise to improve your fret-hand damping: Play the same F barre chord at the first fret again. Hold the chord down solidly, then strum the chord using downstrokes and a steady quarter-note pattern (and later, a faster, eighth-note pattern). Now, using the fret-hand damping technique described above, lift your fret hand slightly off the fretboard between each strum, then press down again before the next strum.

TRACK 30

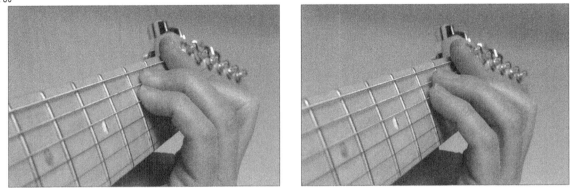

Fret-hand damping (pressure released from strings)

Fret-Hand Finger Damping

You can also use damping to quiet strings next to the strings you're playing. This also comes quite naturally to most players—even when they don't mean to do it! I'm talking about letting your fret-hand fingers brush against and deaden strings next to a fretted string, often with the same finger that is doing the fretting. This often starts out accidentally as a result of poor fret-hand technique—namely by not placing your thumb low enough on the back of the neck to create the proper arch in your fret-hand fingers. If you suffer from this bad habit, you should correct it as soon as possible; there are definite advantages to playing with more accurate, "proper" form. But more advanced players will sometimes knowingly use a little bit of bad form to their advantage as well.

Try this single-note example of fret-hand finger damping: Play C at the fifth fret on the third string with your first finger. Use a downstroke to pick this note, following through with the pick to also strum the second string. Arch your fret-hand finger high so that the second string rings as clearly as the third. Now begin decreasing the arch until the second string buzzes and then is completely deadened by your fret-hand finger. This damping technique is useful in many situations and can be performed by any fret hand finger while playing either single notes or chords.

TRACK 31

Finger damping
(deadening adjacent string)

Fret-Hand Thumb Damping

Speaking of bad form, this is the worst—but everyone does it, so you might as well too. I'm referring to the practice of bringing your fret-hand thumb over the top of the neck to damp the low strings while you play single notes or chords on the higher strings. Watch any Jimi Hendrix video to see this technique displayed in all its glory—just don't let your classical guitar -playing uncle catch you doing it or he's likely to break your thumb off and hand it back to you in his trusty metronome case. Don't worry if your thumb doesn't comfortably reach over the top; the more you play, the more it's likely to creep upward, particularly when you play standing up.

Try this thumb-damping example: Play an open-position D chord—the kind you learned at your first guitar lesson. Strum all six strings and notice that the low E string on your guitar doesn't sound right over the D chord. This is because that note isn't in the chord and doesn't belong there. Now you can just attempt to strum only the top four or five strings (those notes all fit in the D chord) and avoid strumming the low string, or you can simply inch your thumb up slightly over the top of the neck to kill that low string. Then you can strum as wildly as you like without concern for wrong notes. It's easy, and you'll find other places it comes in handy as well.

TRACK 32

Thumb damping (on bottom string)

GET A METRONOME

Metronomes are inexpensive and really mandatory for becoming a solid timekeeper—and no, you won't always be able to depend on a drummer to do that for you. The more you play with a metronome (a drum machine works equally well for this purpose), the more precise your internal clock will become. You should use one of these mechanical "click tracks" with exercises, scales, while reading sheet music, while playing rhythm guitar, or with any tricky guitar part you want to perfect. Try running your metronome through the PA at your next band rehearsal and see how your group measures up against perfect timekeeping. When you're recording your major label debut, chances are the producer will make you do this.

One of the best reasons of all to use a metronome is to help build confidence in your own playing. The metronome serves as a truthful gauge of your progress while learning or polishing difficult pieces of music. Set the device to count slowly until you can play your parts without mistakes (see tip #45 for more on practicing for perfection), then increase the tempo slightly and repeat the part, moving the tempo only slightly higher each time as you sharpen your playing. You'll start to see those metronome settings almost as if they were points on a scoreboard, and you'll gain self-assurance in your playing as you move the numbers higher.

INJECT SOME INTERVALS

There are basically only three really useful things you can play on guitar—single notes, intervals (two notes played simultaneously), and chords (three or more notes played simultaneously). Why then, with those limited options, would you leave out one third of the possibilities by excluding intervallic shapes from your playing? For some strange reason, most players seem to do so.

Intervals—most commonly played as 3rds, 4ths, 5ths, 6ths, or octaves—add a broad range of color that falls squarely between a squealing single note and a chunky chord. They're at home in both solos and rhythm playing, often serving to bridge the gap between the two or to fatten up a guitarist's sound when he's soloing in a trio or other small group setting. Besides that, they just sound cool, and they're fun to play.

The following are some basic intervallic "scales" and riffs to add to your arsenal, using 6ths, octaves, and 3rds. I've decided to leave out 4ths and 5ths since those come naturally to most players anyway. Also, here's one more tip: After you learn some of these riffs or scales, realize that the best use of them may involve playing them modally, particularly in the Mixolydian mode favored by most blues and rock players (if that's your bag), as described in tip #5. Have fun.

Sixths

Sixth interval chord scale, key of E major and based on an open E shape chord (and subsequent barre chords as scale ascends, with root notes on sixth string). The notes played are the 5th and 3rd of each chord:

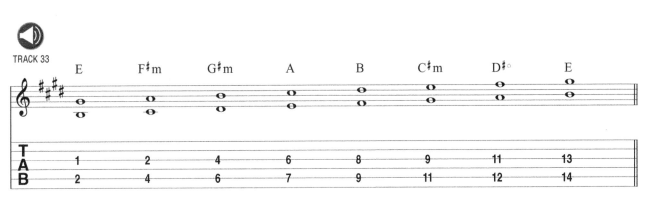

Sixth interval chord scale, key of E major and based on an open E shape chord (and subsequent barre chords). The notes played are the 3rd and root of each chord:

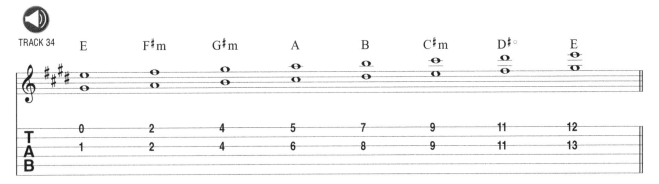

Sixth interval riffs to play over an E–A–B chord progression. These riffs are based on the interval chord scale just shown, with additional chromatic passing tones.

TRACK 35

TRACK 36

Here is a twelve-bar blues in E for you to practice with.

Sixth interval chord scale, key of A major and based on an open A shape chord (and subsequent barre chords as scale ascends, with root notes on fifth string). The notes played are the 5th and 3rd of each chord:

TRACK 37

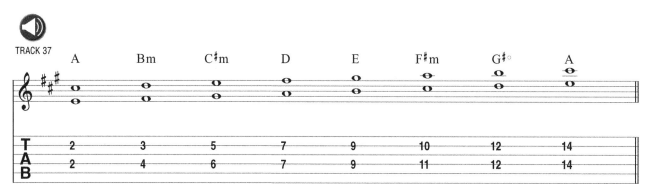

Sixth interval riffs to play over an A–D–E chord progression. These riffs are based on the interval chord scale just shown, with additional chromatic passing tones.

TRACK 38

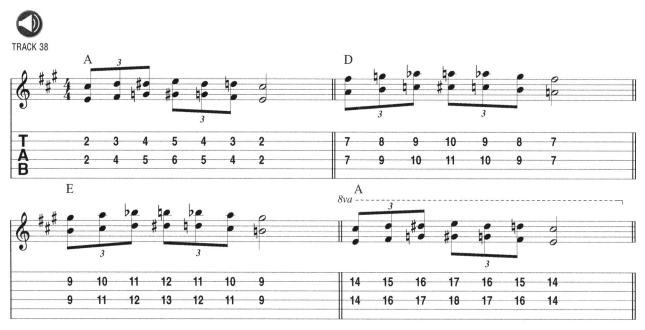

TRACK 39

Here is a twelve-bar blues in A for you to practice with.

Octaves

Octave interval riff, variation one, in E minor. Octaves are played two strings and two frets apart on string sets 6–4 or 5–3.

TRACK 40

Octave interval riff, variation two, in A major: Octaves are played two strings and three frets apart on string sets 4–2 or 3–1.

TRACK 41

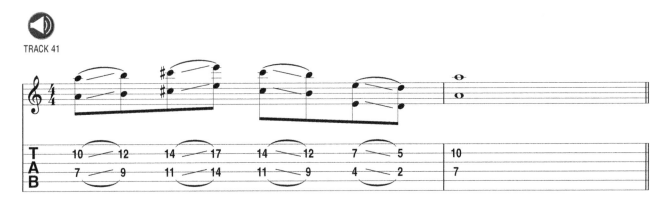

Thirds

Third interval riffs in A major. Practice these over the previous 12-bar blues in A (Track 39).

TRACK 42

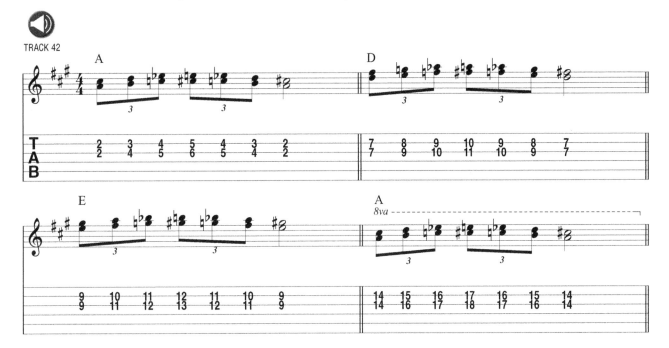

OPEN-STRING SOLOING

Open strings resonate more efficiently than do fretted notes, but many guitarists avoid them, particularly when soloing. They do offer a bit of a challenge, especially because playing down at the nut somewhat hinders use of your index finger, which typically serves as your anchor or pivot anywhere else on the neck.

However, those open strings can be really useful and even raucous when you want them to be, especially after you build up strong hammer-on and pull-off techniques. Of course, the open strings work very well in the key of E, so they fit naturally into many songs in the guitarist's repertoire.

Try these three examples on for size:

Open-string riffs using the E minor pentatonic and E Mixo-Blues scales, à la Stevie Ray Vaughan

TRACK 43

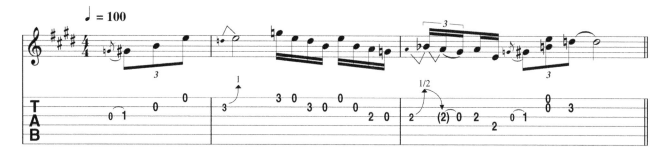

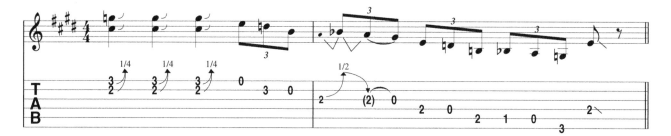

Open-string bounce, fretting a scale up and down the neck on one string, alternating with that string open, à la AC/DC's Angus Young

TRACK 44

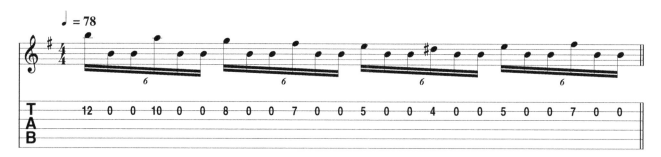

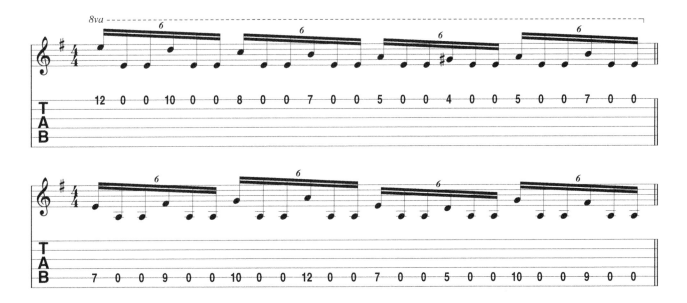

Open-string pull-offs from higher on the neck, à la T-Bone Walker

TRACK 45

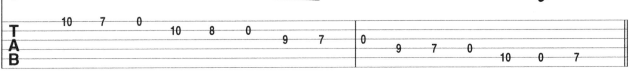

Pick-hand tapping and pull-offs to open strings, à la Edward Van Halen

TRACK 46

*Key signature denotes E Mixolydian.

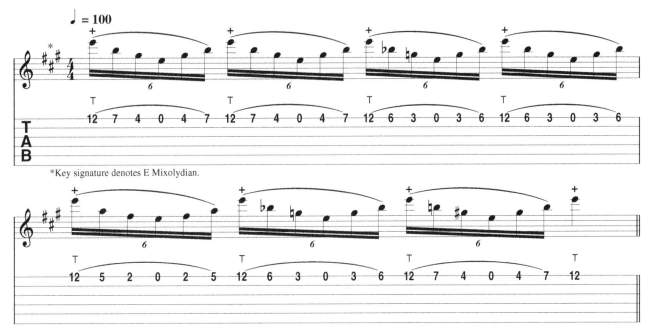

62 HARMONICS

The chimey, harp-like sounds found at numerous places on your fretboard are called harmonics. Harmonics come in two varieties: natural and artificial.

- The easiest to play are *natural harmonics.* Pluck any string while lightly touching that string with your fingertip (don't press down) just above the fourth, fifth, seventh, ninth, or twelfth frets. These are natural harmonics, and they can be played in the same position on each string. You can also play natural harmonics at other locations on the neck, especially between the first and fifth frets, but they're harder to make ring. (Try them on an electric guitar with a lot of gain, distortion, compression, or overdrive.) The following notation shows which frets create which harmonic-note scale interval equivalent. You can use this information to learn the harmonic note names on each string, then add the correct harmonics to your playing, depending on the key of your song.

 Natural harmonics on low E string

TRACK 47

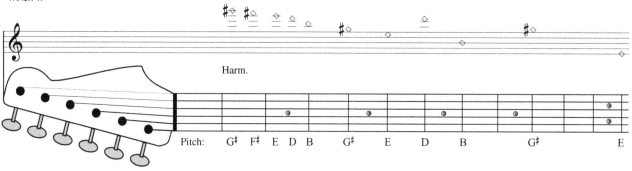

- *Harp harmonics* can be played anywhere on the neck, and while they're slightly tricky to master, they're easy to use in a song because the harmonic name is the same as the note you're fretting. This is because you're always playing the harmonic note twelve frets higher than the fretted note, thus sounding the same note one octave higher. Harp harmonics can be played as single-note patterns or as arpeggios of fretted chords, on either acoustic or electric guitars. As an example, fret and hold a basic open string C chord. With your picking hand, using your thumb to pluck the string, simultaneously touch the fifth string at the fifteenth fret with the tip of your index finger to play the harmonic note C. Don't push down on the string; just touch it lightly. Continue to hold the chord with your fretting hand, then use this same technique to play the harp harmonics of each of the remaining notes in the chord, exactly twelve frets above each fretted note (and at the twelfth fret for any open strings). You can use this technique with any fretted note or chord, anywhere on the neck.

 **Harp harmonics**

TRACK 48

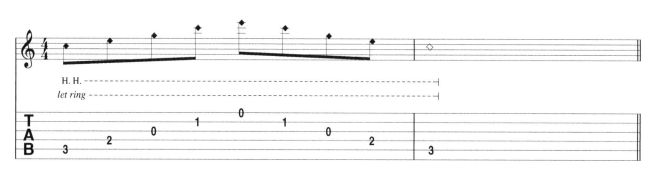

Of course, you can also use natural harmonics as an accurate method of tuning your guitar. Play the harmonic at the fifth fret on the sixth string, then play the harmonic at the seventh fret on the fifth string. These two notes should sound in unison, because they're the same harmonic note. If you hear any wavering of the pitch, adjust your fifth string either sharp or flat until the wavering stops. You'll hear it slowing down as you get close to perfect tuning. If the wavering increases while you're turning the tuning peg, you're going the wrong direction. It helps to actually detune the fifth string a little first, so you know you're starting flat and that you'll have to tune *up* to bring the harmonics into unison. It's always a good practice to tune up, because the strings won't tend to go flat as much when you're bending. Repeat this technique across the rest of the guitar; it works to tune all but the second string. To tune the second string, play the harmonic at the seventh fret on the sixth string, then the second string open (no harmonic, just the open string). You can also use the harmonic at the fifth fret on the sixth string to tune the first string.

63 ALTERNATE TUNINGS

Most of us spend our whole guitar-playing lives in standard tuning. Many top pros, however, including acoustic ace and former Paul McCartney sidekick Laurence Juber and Allman Brothers guitarist Warren Haynes, have told me that they regularly use a variety of open tunings to spur new musical and songwriting ideas. Both of these artists expressed that without even going through the hassle of actually learning how the tuning has moved the notes around on the neck, you'll almost immediately play something new and refreshing just by putting your fingers down in the shape of chords you already know in standard tuning. They refer to these discoveries as "accidental," and that's certainly what they are—happy accidents.

Give it a try with these open tunings (and these are just a handful of all those out there) and see what discoveries you make on your own. And remember, though music theory knowledge is incredibly helpful to your playing, if you put your fingers down on the guitar and good sounds come out, who cares if you know what notes they are! Also note that you may need to put a set of medium or heavy gauge strings on your guitar when using some of these tunings to avoid string buzz.

DADGAD: Probably the most popular alternate tuning of all. Just like it reads, from low to high. DADGAD works especially well for Celtic music, but has been used by everyone from Jimmy Page to Michael Hedges.

Open E: Great for slide playing. From low to high: E–B–E–A–B–E

Open A: From low to high: E–A–E–A–C♯–E. Another great slide tuning.

Open G: From low to high: D–G–D–G–B–D. Keith Richards has made this one famous.

Open D or "Vestapol": From low to high: D–A–D–F♯–A–D

Drop D: A standard for country players, and maybe the easiest first step into alternate tunings. Just drop your low E string a whole step to D. Many modern rock bands tune their entire guitar down a half step or more from standard E tuning, then drop their low E string another whole step to emulate Drop D tuning, albeit far below standard tuning.

Nashville Tuning: Not a tuning, really, but a re-stringing that provides some cool tonal variety for recording session overdubbing. Get a set of strings intended for a 12-string guitar, then just put the thin (higher octave) strings on your six string guitar. String your low E string with the octave string for the low E from the 12-string set. Do the same for the A, D, and G strings. Use a normal B and E string.

64 EXOTIC SCALES

Well-placed exotic scale riffs will knock 'em dead. But they're seemingly so complicated and so far out-side our Western consciousness, they're hard to cement into our memories. Here's some good news: Learn just a couple of simple one-octave patterns to noodle around during the middle of a solo and you'll have everyone worshipping you after the show.

Try these simple samples on for size:

 Whole tone scale in A

TRACK 49

Half/Whole diminished scale in A

TRACK 50

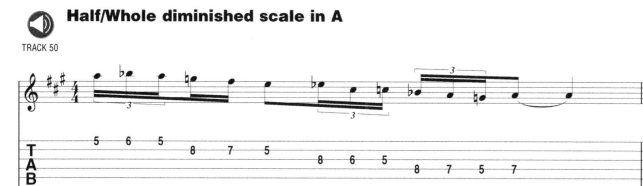

Harmonic minor scale in A

TRACK 51

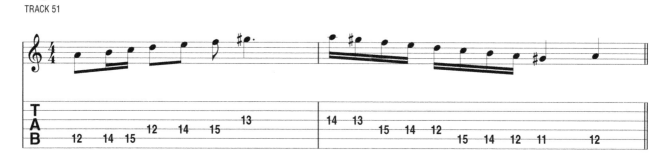

Japanese Iwato scale in A

TRACK 52

Persian scale in A

TRACK 53

65 LIVE EXPERIENCE IS GOLDEN

If you're already a halfway decent musician, you need to get on stage as often as possible, beginning immediately. I've worked with record company A&R execs, critiquing demos and live performances, and I can guarantee you this: You need live experience more than you need another night in the lonely confines of your drummer's basement.

Face it, if you're not playing live, in public, somewhere between 100 and 200 times per year, your stage persona, your in-the-spotlight-charisma, your professional demeanor, is no match even for your neighbor's cousin, the one who plays four nights a week in that shlocky eighties rock cover band, let alone for the potential stars the labels already have their eyes on. And despite that eighties guy's songwriting laziness, if he ever got a few decent tunes together and showcased 'em for a label, it's practically guaranteed they'd take him far more seriously than you. And it's all because he just seems so much more comfortable and professional on stage. And he probably wasn't that pro until something like his 170th show, believe me.

This isn't to say you should give up rehearsing. In fact, you should rehearse as much as possible. But you should take every opportunity to play live no matter the circumstances. As quickly as possible, replace your rehearsals with actual live, in-concert performances. And if you can't get your band booked more than a couple of times a month (like because the only metal club in town will only book you every other week), then start a side-project that plays a completely different type of music and get that band playing live as often as possible. There is no substitute for live experience, and music, being (for most of us) primarily a live kind of thing, is all about how solid, tight, exciting, and passionate your live show is. Entertain us or get off the stage.

CLIMATIC CONDITIONS

Guitars don't want to be too hot or too cold any more than you do, and they'll show their displeasure by warping or cracking if you're not careful. Excessive humidity—or the lack of humidity—will affect your guitars as well, so take precautions. Guitars are best stored in rooms kept between 70 to 75 degrees and at approximately 40 to 50 percent humidity. This is pretty typical of most homes.

If you're keeping your guitars elsewhere—such as a garage, an unfinished basement, storage facility, or rehearsal studio—you should use a thermometer and hygrometer (humidity gauge) to keep tabs on the room's atmospheric conditions. If your guitars are being exposed to chilling cold or scalding heat, and it's not feasible or doesn't make economic sense to bring in a heater or air conditioner (and keep it running even when you're not there), you'll have to move them somewhere else before they're damaged. Also be aware that allowing the sun to shine on your guitars, even as it passes by a window, can ruin the finish of the guitar and compromise the guitar's construction.

Luckily, solving the humidity issue is easier. You can run a humidifier or vaporizer—or even place open containers of water near your instruments—to add moisture to the air when necessary. The small humidifiers that are made to soak, then place in a guitar's case with the guitar, are very effective tools for fighting drying, cracking conditions. (But they don't do much good if you don't remember to re-moisten them from time to time—and they can ruin your guitar's finish if you let them leak.) If too much moisture is a problem, you can put small silica gel packages—the kind that come inside the packing material of almost any electronic device—in your guitar case.

Remember that even in your home, where the temperature may stay in the same comfortable range year round, the humidity may change drastically between summer and winter. Furnaces, in particular, can dry the air in your home considerably, negatively affecting your guitars. Though we all like to display our guitars out in the open, keeping them in their cases is actually the best thing we can do to protect them from adverse conditions.

Also, if you take your guitar out in the winter cold, then bring it into a heated building, let it warm up inside the case for awhile before taking it out. Allowing the guitar to warm up too quickly after being very cold could cause checking in the finish. In the frigid cold of winter, think about warming up your car before you bring your guitar out. Remember to do the opposite in summer—cool off the car with the air conditioner before you load up. And never put your guitar in the trunk. Your heater and air conditioner can't help it back there, and rattling around with your spare tire and lug wrench won't do your case any favors either.

 FINGERTIPS AND NAILS

Your fingertips and fingernails (if you're into fingerpicking styles of guitar playing) are obviously extremely important to your tone and overall playing. Cracked nails and torn-up calluses are really a pain, both literally and figuratively. In many cases, the simple solution lies in a little bottle at your local hardware or drug store.

Stevie Ray Vaughan routinely used Super Glue to re-attach calluses that he had worn off—sometimes even taking a razor blade to the callus to reshape it before re-attaching it to the damaged fingertip. Now I don't personally recommend getting anywhere near your fingertips with either razor blades or Super Glue, but if you've got a really important gig, and you've got a problem with a callus that's about to come off… Alternately, you could, of course, try fingertip or spot bandages. Also, liquid bandage products such as Nu-Skin may solve your problem, at least temporarily.

A more useful tip regarding nail care comes from the ranks of hot studio session players in Nashville. I've heard more than one say they use clear liquid nail hardeners—the kind you find in the cosmetics section of your local drugstore, next to the nail polish—to keep their picking hand fingernails from tearing, cracking, or just wearing out. They also sculpt their nails to optimum length and shape (both of which are subject to need and personal taste) with emery boards or nail files. Now I like beer and football as much as the next guy, but if I were making a six-figure salary fingerpicking a steel-stringed acoustic in a recording studio five or six days a week, and my fingernails weren't up to the task, I'd be buying the emery boards and Hot & Sexy nail hardener by the case. How about you?

Of course, if you're a female guitarist, you've got no problem purchasing these items. If you're a guy, however, and you can't bring yourself to walk into a store and purchase nail care products, ask the woman in your life to help you out, or buy them online. A few words of caution: If you're going to use the liquid hardener on a regular basis, be aware that formaldehyde (a common ingredient in many nail hardeners) will dry out your nails over time, causing them to become brittle. It can also cause allergic reactions in some people. Search for brands of nail hardener that contain less than 3 percent formaldehyde, and follow the directions.

 CHANGE ONE STRING AT A TIME

Guitars, at their very core, are a balancing act between the pressure exerted by tightly stretched steel strings, and the resistance to that pressure provided by the (usually) wooden body and neck. Yes, most guitar necks are supported by a steel truss rod, but it too is adjusted for optimal tension *with* a full set of in-tune strings. When you remove all your guitar strings before putting the new strings on, you present the guitar—the body, the neck, the truss rod—with a sudden and very drastic change in tension.

When you then put a new set of strings on the guitar the pressure resumes, and the body, neck, and truss rod must readjust. This relaxation and resumption of tension can potentially throw the guitar out of whack, messing up your intonation, your truss rod adjustment, or the alignment of your neck and body (particularly with bolt-on necks). At the very least, it may take your guitar longer to re-stabilize and stay in tune.

It's far better to remove and replace one string at a time when changing guitar strings, beginning with your lowest, heaviest gauge strings. This minimizes the variation in tension during the process. Heed this advice and your guitar will spend far less time out of tune, out of intonation, or in the repair shop. For more information on truss rod adjustments, see tip #85.

 69 CORICIDAN BOTTLE BLUES

Allman Brothers guitarist Warren Haynes recently told me that his slide of choice is the trusty old Coricidan bottle (once an actual medicine bottle but now sold in most music stores as a guitar slide). That's the same slide that Warren's predecessor, Duane Allman, used in the legendary group that bears his and brother Gregg's name.

But Warren also keeps a second slide (a glass slide with an open end) on stage, because on a long sweaty night, the close-ended Coricidan bottle becomes so humid that his calluses soften and sometimes even come off. Warren says he might have someone drill small holes in the closed end of the slide to let the moisture out, preserving his calluses for when he's fretting the guitar without the slide. Though this sounds like it should work, we also discussed putting a small cotton ball in the slide as well, which would be easier than drilling (though possibly not as effective at reducing humidity).

 70 GET TOOLED UP

There are endless situations in which you *might* need a tool during a gig. And "might" is the key word, because 99 percent of the time you'll never need any of this stuff. And then...

And then that one night will come along—and it's likely to be a really important night, if Murphy's Law holds true—when you'll *really* need a spare fuse for your amp, or an extension cord to reach that far-away electrical outlet, or a ground tap to eliminate that dreadful hum coming through your rig, or a screwdriver to fix a strap holder that has just given out, or... You name it, the technical catastrophes that can ruin your big night on stage are seemingly endless, and they're usually extremely minor issues, making them all the more aggravating when you can't correct them and get on with your gig or session.

So be prepared and put together a took kit containing the following items:

- Small and medium size screwdrivers, both Phillips and slot.
- A small crescent wrench or pair of pliers, particulary Vice Grips—your drummer will really thank you for these.
- A pair of needlenose pliers.

- Appropriately sized Allen wrenches—particularly if you're using a floating bridge, such as a Floyd Rose.

- Wire cutters/wire strippers.

- Electrical tape and duct tape.

- An extension cord—I've only occasionally needed one, but usually bring at least a 25-footer.

- A power strip—a must if you have a lot of rack effects or pedals requiring AC adapters. Also a necessity when you find out the club owner won't let you unplug a single one of his twenty-three neon beer signs so you can fire up your PA.

- A ground lift (the thing that adapts your amp's power cord from a three-pronged problem into a two-pronged solution).

- Spare fuses, fuse caps, or tubes for your amp—check the size or type before you need them and buy the appropriate replacements as spares, don't cheat and risk ruining your gear. And don't underestimate your ability to smash your fuse caps while carrying your gear into a club, rendering your amplifier useless.

- Fresh spare batteries—9-volt and any others your various devices might require.

- A small- or medium-sized flashlight (even on a well-lit stage, the inside of your amp or back of your guitar is likely to be too dark to work on.)

- A string winder—which will really speed up the removal and replacement of a broken string at a critical moment. (This is especially helpful if you don't have a backup guitar.)

- A soldering iron and solder—for more serious repairs that you probably should have done at home before the gig anyway, or for fixing a broken cord between sets.

- A bar towel or polishing rag—you'll need this in a hurry if some moron spills a drink on your valuable or electrified stuff.

- Band-Aids.

- And spares of everything else you might need, particularly strings, a guitar strap, and a couple of extra cords (both long and short).

Of course, it helps if you know how to use each of these items before the emergency breaks. Schedule time to take care of routine maintenance on your guitar, amp, effects, rack, pedal board, and PA before you get to the club or studio and you'll not only save yourself needless stress, you'll also learn how to properly use everything in your tool kit. This brand of knowledge will benefit you far beyond your on-stage endeavors, like when your van breaks down in the middle of New Mexico on your next cross-country tour, and the only mechanic within 100 miles is you.

TUBE REPLACEMENT SCHEDULE

Don't wait until you hear them go. You won't hear them (unless your amp just suddenly dies altogether). More than likely, your tone will gradually get worse and worse, and you'll be going out of your mind trying to figure out if it's your tubes or your ears. Face it, just like a light bulb, your tubes are dying from the second you first fire them up. Just plan on replacing them on a certain calendar date, maybe on your birthday or some other memorable annual occasion, and you'll be guaranteed a reliable, consistent amplifier tone.

Pros generally replace their tubes once or twice a year, if not more often (though they may be playing more than you, which certainly quickens the decay of their tone). Renowned guitar tech Rene Martinez told me that, when he's on the road with Carlos Santana, he changes tubes about once a month. You may decide to change out your power tubes every other year, if money is an issue. But at an average price of $40 per set, changing tubes once a year shouldn't be out of anyone's budget.

And also, if you buy what are referred to as "matched pairs," such as those sold by Groove Tubes, you probably won't have to worry about having someone bias your amp with the new tubes (refer to your amp's owner's manual, or the manufacturer's website), though it's a good idea to have the amp biased if possible. Biasing insures that your amp is getting even output from each tube; one tube isn't working harder than the other, which can eventually damage your amplifier. Note that some amps today are "self-biasing."

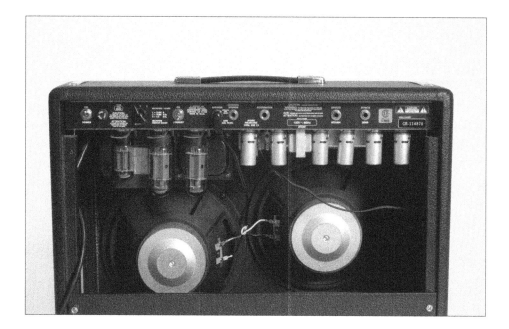

72 INSURE YOUR INVESTMENT

If you never play your guitar outside of your own home and you live in the high-rent part of Malibu, you'll probably assess your homeowner's or renter's insurance needs differently than the struggling, gonna-be guitar hero sharing his one-bedroom apartment just off Hollywood and Vine with a couple of former, disgruntled bandmates and a revolving cast of less-than-trustworthy exotic dancers. And especially if you're out and about with your prized possessions on a regular basis, do not underestimate or deny the possibility—probability even—that sooner or later, you will have something stolen from your car, your pad, or even right off the stage. It's happened to me all three ways, and I've always been highly security-conscious.

If you own a home, chances are your mortgage lender requires that you have homeowner's insurance, which will cover you even when away from home with your gear. But many guitarists pursuing the dream of musical success are renters, often with low-paying day jobs and no insurance. If this describes you, you'd probably be surprised to find out how inexpensive renter's insurance can be. Typically, it covers your equipment even when you take it out of your residence, such as to a studio or club. You might even be able to add it on to your auto insurance bill, which would allow you to spread out the payments over twelve months and would typically add only a few dollars to your monthly nut. And the insurance will more than pay for itself the first time you lose even a medium-priced guitar, which the company will pay you to replace.

Now, neither I, nor most financial planners, advocate paying for "preventative coverage" such as extended warranties on products you buy, because you can usually guarantee that you're not going to break the item. But no one can guarantee 100 percent that some other loser isn't going to steal their guitar some lousy night. Consequently, an inexpensive renter's insurance policy will always prove to be either a good investment, or at the very least, peace of mind. Most major insurance companies offer renter's insurance policies, and some even offer other types of policies specifically intended to indemnify musical instruments and other professional equipment—especially if you can prove that you're making money by playing music. Rate quotes are probably no further than a phone call or a few Internet clicks away. Don't delay; your victimization could be only a band break-up or broken heart away.

73 HAZARDOUS MATERIALS

Strumming an acoustic guitar and singing the songs of our youth with my family and friends around a high-mountain campfire is a particular fantasy of mine. Maybe it's yours, too. If so, a word of caution: Do not allow a single drop of insect repellent to come into contact with your guitar. It will melt your finish like a bonfire melts marshmallows. The same goes for liquid fire starters we commonly use with the barbecue—or basically any petroleum product, for that matter. And for the more urban picker, watch out for your girl's nail polish remover (or your own nail polish remover, if that's what you're into). Some repair experts even suggest that Lemon Pledge and other such furniture polishes with lemon extract (citric acid) could potentially harm certain guitars (see tip #83).

Getting your guitar or amp from place to place usually involves no more than a short automotive trip. When your gear is about to join the mile-high club, however, more serious precautions are called for. Tips #74 through 77 cover flying and shipping your valued instruments in safety.

74 FLYING WITH YOUR GUITAR

The days are pretty much gone when you can plan to carry your guitar on an airplane like you can a backpack or garment bag (even though many guitar cases are smaller than most garment bags—and this discrimination really irks me). So here's a tip: Don't check your guitar at the curb or ticket counter. Carry it with you to the gate and try to bring it on the plane like it's no big deal. Using a gig bag helps here, as they're smaller than a typical hard shell case. Arrive in time to board the plane early, before the businessmen fill up the closets with their garment bags.

If the flight crew just won't let you carry it on, check the guitar right before you board the plane. Not only does this allow you to get in a little extra practice while waiting for your flight, it insures that your instrument will be treated much more gently by the baggage handlers. When you check a bag at the gate, it is typically hand-carried down to the cargo area of the plane by the baggage crew manager or flight attendant, avoiding the typical rough handling and throwing endured by mere suitcases, courtesy of the lowly pack mules.

And when your flight is over, don't run straight to baggage claim. Wait in the jetway just outside the door of the plane, and you'll get your guitar back before all the passengers have even emptied the overheads. The senior baggage handler will promptly hand-deliver the instrument to you right there, avoiding the dangers of the baggage carousel, which include both damage *and* theft.

75 EVEN IN A FLIGHT CASE...

I recently flew my favorite combo amp across country for a couple of out-of-town gigs and had the shock of literally watching the baggage handlers casually *toss* my very large and heavy Anvil-type case into the airplane. I swear I heard the ugly thud from my window seat above the plane's cargo door. When we arrived at our destination, the amp wouldn't make a sound. Upon this discovery, I had to frantically find a repair shop to analyze and correct the problem—and just a couple of hours before the gig. The diagnosis: Due to the rough handling, my channel switching/reverb foot pedal, which I normally keep in the back of the combo amp wrapped in its own cord, had rattled around and crushed both speaker cones in my amp. The speakers had to be replaced on the spot.

Many musicians use the open back of their combo amp as a carrying case for assorted items. I commonly see players stowing effects pedals, microphones, or small took kits back there. My costly and stressful experience taught me that, even inside an expensive and virtually indestructible flight case, your amp can be damaged by loose items rattling around, especially in the hands of less-than-concerned airline baggage handlers or moving company employees. You're probably fine using your amp as an oversized effects pedal carrying case from gig to gig, but clear out any unfastened stuff before you put your amp or rack unit in the hands of the Neanderthals at the airport.

If you're shipping your guitar somewhere, consider protecting both the instrument and its case by placing them inside a box well-stuffed with newspaper, bubble wrap, or other packing materials. If you don't have a suitable box, go to your nearest music store and ask for boxes from a recent shipment of guitars. They'll usually be happy to hand them over free of charge, and you'll be adding an additional element of protection to your valued friend.

If you keep your guitar in a gig bag or other such soft case, put something else in the cardboard box along with the guitar and packing materials for added support and protection, such as a piece of plywood or even another stiff cardboard box, folded to fit. Also, it's a good idea to loosen the tension on your strings and support your guitar's neck and headstock with crumpled newspaper or bubble wrap. And don't leave loose stuff free to hop or slide around inside your case (stuff the in-case storage space full of newspaper, after putting its contents in a sealed bag). Guitars can be damaged even inside a case if handled improperly. All of the above holds true for amps, too. Pack 'em up securely, and everything should be all right.

And don't forget to insure! No insurance = no claim = tough luck, loser.

I hope you'll never experience the misfortune of having your guitar or amp stolen. But if you do, you'll wish that, in addition to having the items properly insured (as discussed in tip #72), you had taken a few simple precautions that might aid in their recovery. The most obvious is to have the serial number and original store receipt tucked away in a safe place. Additionally, you should have photos of the gear, including close-ups of any distinctive adornments (unique inlays, autographs, etc.), blemishes or damage (nicks and scratches, burns, etc.), after market add-ons (tremolo bars, pickups, electronics, etc.), or anything else that makes the guitar unique.

And for an added bit of help in recovering a stolen item, in the event it should fall into the hands of the police or some other good Samaritan, you should put your name and contact info somewhere inside the instrument or amp. Make sure you don't damage the instrument while doing this—you probably don't want to carve your initials into a perfectly good guitar with a pocketknife or anything foolish like that. And remember that serial numbers and other exterior identifiers can easily be removed or altered.

There are a number of useful options, however. You can engrave your name and social security number inside a guitar's pickup cavity. Chances are the thief will never look inside, but the police will, if you ask them to do so. You can also write your contact info on an adhesive label, then stick it up inside the guitar through a sound hole or ƒ-hole, or on the inside of an amplifier or speaker cabinet, out of site to the casual observer, where it can be seen only by using a small jeweler's or dentist's mirror. Think like a thief to out-think them, don't cause any damage, and do what it takes to get yourself some added peace of mind.

Most pro guitar techs—the guys and girls out there installing new strings on several guitars before every show by your favorite rock stars—use the same technique for winding new strings onto a guitar's tuning posts. Their technique reduces string slippage and keeps the celeb's guitars in better tune. It seems tricky at first, but it's really quite simple.

Step 1: Put the string straight through the hole in the tuning post, with no bend in the string's path.

Step 2: Manually (not using the tuning pegs) wind the string end half way around the tuning post, bringing it under the string. Wind clockwise for the three bass strings on a three-on-a-side headstock (Les Paul, etc.) and counter-clockwise for the three treble strings. Wind all the strings clockwise on a straight-six style headstock (Strat, Tele, etc.).

Step 3: Bend the string end up and over the string, reversing the direction you were winding, with the bend tight up against the string and tuning post. Crease this bend with your thumb or index finger if necessary.

Step 4: Tune the guitar using the tuning pegs. The bend will now make a half-hitch knot in your string, and you'll stay in tune longer and more reliably. Of course, you should always turn the tuning pegs away from the body of the guitar, regardless what type of tuning peg arrangement (straight-six or three-on-a-side) you have.

Run the string straight through the tuning post.

Wind the string halfway around the tuning post.

Bend the string up and over itself.

Turn the pegs to tune the guitar as usual.

12-string guitars can really be tough to play, but they add such a gorgeous, harpsichord-like quality to your sonic palette that you really owe it to yourself to pick one up. The big question for new 12-string players is always the same: Do the octave strings belong before or after the fundamental strings? Realize this is only an issue for the low E, A, D, and (sometimes) G strings, which have a wound, full gauge string and an unwound, higher octave string in each pair. The B, and high E strings come in unison pairs of unwound strings.

When stringing a 12-string, you'll want to put the unwound, higher-octave string from each pair of strings *before* the wound, full-size string, from low to high on the guitar. The twelfth string should be the high octave of the wound, low E string, which should itself be placed in the eleventh position on the guitar. The higher octave A string should be in tenth position, with the wound A string in ninth. The higher octave D string should be in the eighth position, with the wound D string in seventh. The unwound G string should be in the sixth position, with the wound G string in the fifth position.

This method of string arrangement on a 12-string insures that your pick or fingers will connect with each string in each pair as you strum or fingerpick. If the strings were put on the guitar with each of the wound strings placed ahead of its unwound, higher octave, your pick and fingers will tend to skip over the higher octave string, robbing you of half the effect of playing this beautiful instrument.

Sometimes friction between the strings and the nut causes a "ping" sound when we tune. It's as if the string is binding and releasing in the nut as you turn the tuning peg—and binding is exactly what the string is doing. This friction may cause your guitar to tune erratically and/or cause difficulties in keeping the guitar in tune while playing. Almost any guitar, but particularly acoustics, can be made to tune more accurately (and play better as well), by adding a little graphite to the nut. And it's as easy as sharpening a pencil.

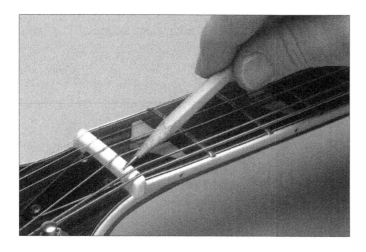

Pencil "lead" is actually graphite. The next time you replace your strings, take a pencil, shave off a little bit of the graphite tip (chop it up if you must, to make a fine powder), then put a few grains of this powder in each string slot on the nut of your guitar before replacing the strings. You can try just rubbing the pencil point in the nut slot, but most pencil tips are too big to fit all the way down. Repeat this process at the bridge if you use a tremolo system. You don't have to do this every time you change strings, but frequent addition of more graphite will only help keep your strings from binding, and it can't hurt your guitar.

Tuning up should now be effortless and without the creaking and pinging caused by binding strings. If you would rather not harm any cute little pencils in the process, you can ask your local music store for a product called GraphitAll (or order it direct from famous guitar tech Rene Martinez at www.texasguitarwhiz. com). You can also purchase powdered graphite lubricant at any auto parts store, though one container will be far more than a lifetime supply. Then again, it will come in handy the next time the key sticks in the ignition of your new Ferrari.

81 GRINDS, NOT GROANS

The concept of having someone crown or replace your frets can be plenty scary to novice players. Just the mention of it evokes images of major surgery and bills rivaling those of a lengthy hospital stay. However, fret jobs are not as big of a deal as many guitarists make them out to be, and they're not as expensive as you might think. Regular fret care will almost certainly improve the playability of your instrument, if not your playing itself.

When you're playing guitar, you're typically grinding metal strings against metal frets, hour after hour, day after day, week after week. Face it: Frets wear out. If you're like many guitarists, especially rock guitarists, you'll see worn spots on your second, fifth, and seventh frets (particularly if you spend a lot of time playing in E or in that trusty old A minor pentatonic scale). Worn frets can make it harder to tune your guitar, and they make anything you play that involves those worn frets sound out of tune—chords, single notes, bends, you name it.

If you're suffering from worn frets, get over the fear and take your guitar to a reputable repair shop ASAP. It should cost only about $40 to $60 to "crown" or smooth out the worn frets. And the repair person won't just fix the affected areas, they'll do what they must to make all your frets conform to very exact tolerances, improving playability from top to bottom. This is, of course, done mostly by grinding and therefore might slightly alter the setup of your guitar. Your frets will be slightly lower or smaller after this process—we're basically talking microns here—which means you may be able to lower your action slightly (if that's important to you). And even if you're spending six hours a day playing the same guitar, you'll probably only need to have this done a time or two per guitar in your lifetime.

At some point, however, a guitar's frets may become so worn or may have been ground down enough times that they must be replaced to bring the guitar back into playing shape. As frightening as this might sound, it's really a pretty simple operation for a qualified repair person and will probably cost no more than $150, which may be pocket change compared to replacing that particular instrument. On average, you can probably have your frets crowned at least three times before you'll have to replace them.

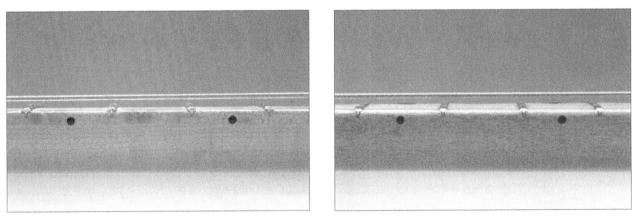

New frets   Worn frets

Despite decades of playing, I've never yet had to re-fret a guitar. Steve Howe, the virtuoso guitarist of Yes, told me recently that he has never re-fretted his main guitar, a trusty 1964 Gibson ES-175—which he bought new—even after decades of recording and touring.

82 SRV BROKEN-STRING SOLUTION

We all break strings from time to time. This is especially true if we're playing on an older, worn set or on a guitar that hasn't been serviced in awhile or set up properly. But Stevie Ray Vaughan had his strings changed before every show, and his guitars were serviced daily by one of the best in the business—and he still managed to break at least one string pretty much every night.

Stevie's long-time guitar tech, Rene Martinez, told me that he came upon a solution to Stevie's problem one day while sucking on a lollipop and stringing Stevie's guitars before a concert. The lollipop had a plastic tube, like a thin straw. Rene hit upon the idea of inserting Stevie's strings through that plastic tubing, then sliding the tubing up through the block of Stevie's Strat tremolo bar and up through the bridge hole, then running the strings over the saddle as usual. The plastic tube protected Stevie's strings from creasing and eventually snapping on rough or sharp edges inside the bridge, behind the saddle—the

usual break point. When Stevie then went fifteen shows in a row without breaking a string, Rene knew he'd found his solution.

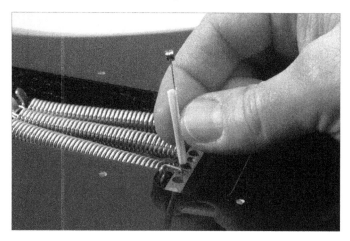

You can do the same with thin plastic tubing often available at electronic or crafts stores—or even a drinking straw that's been split open and trimmed to fit. Some small coffee stirrers or mixed drink straws are actually tubular and just about the right size, though they may require a little bending before they become flexible enough to do the job. They may not work on your thicker, low-end strings, but those strings don't break as often anyway.

83 CLEANING THE BODY & NECK

The finish on your guitar should be important to you, particularly if it's a collectible item and you want the guitar to increase in value over time. And if you think your guitar isn't worth much now, keep in mind that all the people who bought cheap guitars after they saw the Beatles on Ed Sullivan are wishing they still had those cheap guitars now, because some of them are worth tens of thousands of dollars today. Almost everything becomes a collectible a couple of decades later—so take care of your guitar!

Elbow grease is the main ingredient for keeping your guitar clean and the finish in good condition. The other tools you need include only a soft, lint free cloth (t-shirts and cotton flannel work well) and some guitar polish/cleaner or naptha (lighter fluid). If your guitar is particularly dirty with caked-on grime use a small amount of naptha on your cleaning rag. If the guitar is only mildly dirty or dusty, try to clean it with just the dry cloth or go straight to the polish/cleaner. Wrap the cloth tightly around your index finger or into a tight ball held in the palm of your hand for best results.

A trustworthy brand is Martin Guitar Polish, sold at any music store that carries Martin guitars. Another useful polish is called Mirror Glaze Swirl Remover #9, sold in auto parts stores for putting fine finishes on cars. Most furniture polishes will work too, though some experts feel polish with lemon may potentially harm the finish of a guitar, especially if the instrument already has any checking (small cracks that sometimes form with age).

If you don't have any polish on hand, your warm breath will work almost as well. You can also dampen your cloth in a little warm water, but be careful around the electronics of an electric guitar or any place where the finish has been compromised. Optimally, you'll lean as much as possible toward cleaning your guitar with a totally dry cloth before you start adding cleaning solutions, especially if your guitar is vintage. Try to use the polish and cleaning solutions only occasionally. All cleaning products will eventually penetrate the finish and end up in the wood of the guitar, which may affect the tone as the instrument ages.

84 CLEANING THE FRETBOARD

In most cases, your fretboard probably needs only an occasional wipe down with a soft, dry cloth. Use your fingernail or a guitar pick to press the cloth into the edges of the frets where grime builds. If your fretboard is seriously dirty, you should first soften any hardened grime with a small amount of naptha on a cloth or Q-tip. Scrape the grime off with something that won't cut into the wood. A credit card or heavy guitar pick will work well in this situation.

A very fine 0000 steel wool can be used, pinched between your thumb and fingers, to clean and polish the frets, fret-fretboard joints, and in fact, the entire fretboard. Rub lightly and in one direction only, with the grain of the wood, so as not to leave any unsightly marks. A small dab of lemon oil on the fretboard will keep the wood from becoming too dry and cracking.

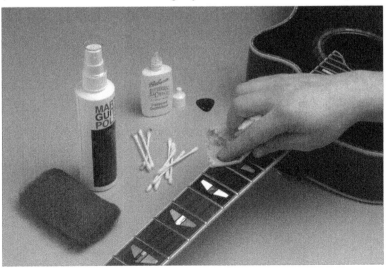

A word of caution: If your guitar has a maple (blond) neck, don't use steel wool or lemon oil. You'll have to stick to a soft cloth to avoid removing the clear lacquer coat most manufacturers put on maple necks.

All guitars need routine set-up maintenance. Tips #85 through 87 describe the most common adjustments: truss rod, action, and intonation. Always adjust them in that order if you must make any changes to the truss rod or the action. Truss rod adjustments affect action, and both of those affect intonation.

85 TRUSS ROD ADJUSTMENTS

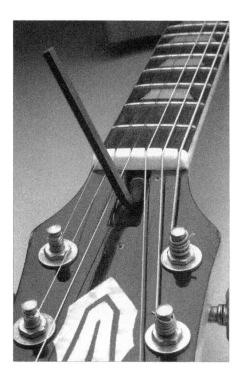

If your guitar is fretting out (your strings are buzzing in certain places on the neck), or if your action is too high, you may need to adjust your truss rod. The truss rod is a metal bar that runs through the middle of the guitar's neck and is accessible at one end or the other of the fretboard, possibly under a cap (such as on a Les Paul) or inside the body of an acoustic guitar. You'll need the appropriate tool to adjust the truss rod, which may be an Allen wrench, a socket/nut driver, or a screwdriver.

Before adjusting your truss rod, sight down the neck from the headstock to the body and determine if you neck has an up-bow (with the guitar laid flat on its back, the neck would bow upward) or back-bow. Most guitars need a slight up-bow (referred to as *relief*) to play with a minimum of buzzing. Too much up-bow, however, and the action will be so high the guitar will be difficult to play. Too much back-bow, and strings will be fretting out all over the place.

If your guitar has too much up-bow, tighten the truss rod by turning it clockwise. Turn the truss rod counterclockwise to reduce back-bow. A quarter to a half-turn should be plenty. If you go beyond that, you're probably going too far. If the truss rod begins to squeak, stop turning; it can't go anymore.

If there is a hump in your fretboard, usually where the neck meets the body, or if the tongue rises (the part of the fretboard that hovers over or is attached to the body), you may need professional help with your guitar.

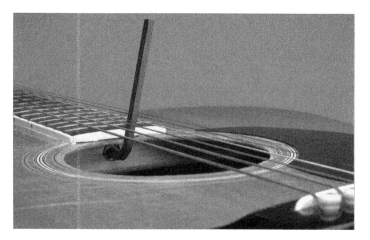

How your guitar feels when you play it, and particularly the height of the strings off the neck, is referred to as "action." Some players like very low action; some prefer higher action, allowing them to dig into the strings a little harder. It's all a matter of personal taste, though musical style often dictates your action. If you're into extreme speed, for example, lower is better.

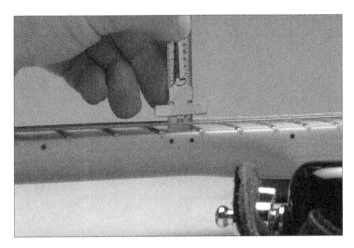

The simple way to adjust the action on an electric guitar is to raise or lower the bridge by turning the screws that adjust the bridge height or the height of the individual bridge saddles. Purchase an inexpensive machinist's ruler from a hardware store and measure from the top of the twelfth fret to the bottom of your sixth (or seventh) string. Adjust the height of the bridge or bridge saddle until this gap measures 3/32 of an inch. Take the same measurement on your first string and adjust the bridge until that gap measures 2/32 of an inch. The strings in between should fall somewhere in the middle of these two measurements. These tolerances are meant to serve as a good starting point, from which you may want to raise or lower your action slightly.

Also note that the height of your bridge or bridge saddles must take into account the radius (curvature) of your guitar neck. The more the curvature of your neck, the more the bridge saddles in the middle will need to be raised to keep your action consistent across all your strings. A Gibson-style "Tune-O-Matic" bridge is built with its own radius, matching that of the guitar neck. A Fender-style bridge, with individual bridge saddle height adjustment screws, is not. (Most other manufacturer bridges are modeled after one or the other of these two industry standards.)

Gibson-style "Tune-O-Matic" bridge

Fender-style bridge

Acoustic guitar action is a tougher adjustment to make and should probably be left to a pro repairperson. It typically involves removing the bridge saddle from the guitar and either shaving it slightly on the bottom or adding a shim under it. Potentially, adjustments to the bridge itself and/or the nut will also be necessary.

Another factor in unsatisfactory action on either electric or acoustic guitars could be improper truss rod adjustment, which may also show other symptoms such as fret buzz or an obviously warped neck. See tip #85 for more information on adjusting your truss rod.

87 SETTING INTONATION

It's easy to set your own intonation, saving yourself $20 to $40 each time you don't take your guitar to a shop—and a lot of mental anguish over how the guitar can play in tune one place on the neck and out of tune another. Setting your intonation refers to making an adjustment of the length of the string from the bridge to the nut. Required tools include only a screwdriver and a tuner, and you'll need to locate the screws that move your bridge saddles back and forth.

Plug your guitar into your tuner, tune up your low E string, then play E at the twelfth fret. If the note is sharp, lengthen the string by turning the saddle adjustment screw counterclockwise, moving the bridge saddle away from the neck. If the note is flat, turn the screw clockwise to move the bridge saddle toward the neck, shortening the string.

Tune the string again, and repeat the process until the note at the twelfth fret plays in tune. Repeat these steps for each string. With a little practice, you'll be able to intonate the whole guitar in about fifteen minutes.

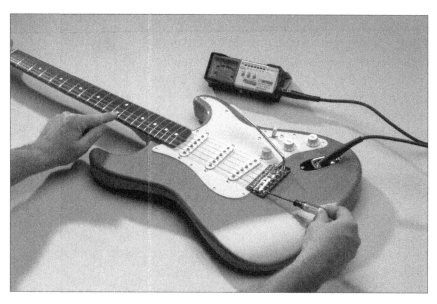

One thing to understand, however: A guitar is what is known as an even-tempered instrument. Guitars are made to play "generally" in tune in all keys, but not perfectly in tune in any one key. Accept this as fact and save yourself from the loony bin.

 LOCKING TUNERS

Life is so much easier when you've got locking tuners—those made by Sperzel or any similar product—on your electric guitar. Unless you're playing a rare or vintage instrument, consider replacing your tuners with the locking variety. With locking tuners, when you put a new string on your guitar, there's no more wrapping, no more pricking your fingers, and no more bloody headstocks. You just put the string through the little hole in the tuning post and lock it down with a twist of your wrist, then tune.

 TIPS 89 – 92: YOU GOT ME FLOATING

Floating bridges, most notably the Floyd Rose tremolo system, can be a lot of fun. They can also be a huge hassle. The most troublesome aspect of floating bridge systems is that, when you break a string, you're out of tune immediately—drastically out of tune. There is no way around this dilemma; it's the nature of the invention. Tips #89 and 90 explain precautions to avoid broken strings on a floater and what to do when you need to replace them. Tips #91 and 92 explain a few other adjustments that will make playing with the bridge less problematic and more enjoyable.

 AVOIDING BROKEN STRINGS
ON A FLOATING BRIDGE

The best way to avoid broken strings while using a floating bridge is much the same as on any other bridge system: Change your strings regularly and don't play too rough. New strings have more elasticity than older, stretched out strings and are less likely to snap. Also, you should occasionally treat the nut and bridge saddles with graphite as described in tip #80. If you're playing a really important gig (aren't they all?), have a second guitar tuned up and ready to go. If you do break a string while performing, just dive bomb out, turn the volume off, and quickly change guitars. Practice switching guitars mid-song at rehearsal.

Just like most traditional tremolo systems, a floating bridge tremolo unit balances the guitar strings against a set of springs inside a body cavity accessible through the back of the guitar. But unlike traditional tremolo systems, which are usually attached to the body of the guitar with bolts or screws, the entirely free-floating bridge itself acts as a fulcrum. It's not secured to the body of the guitar at all. If you were to remove all the strings at once or detach the springs, the bridge would fall right out of the guitar. Do I even have to say it? Don't do this!

Because of the very sensitive balance struck between the strings and springs on a floating bridge, you'll want to change strings one at a time, completely retuning each string—including stretching it out several times, then retuning again—before you remove the next string. Follow these steps:

- Unlock the nut and bridge saddle for the broken or dead string and remove it. You may have to pull a small piece of broken string out of the bridge itself, after unlocking the bridge saddle clamp. If you can't get the broken fragment out by hand or by tipping the guitar upside down and shaking lightly, use a pair of needlenose pliers or tweezers. You must remove any broken string ends or the bridge may not lock down securely on the new string. Sometimes, the pieces are small and hard to see. Use a flashlight if necessary.

- Clip the ball off the end of the new string to insert the string into the bridge saddle clamp or run the string backward (with the ball end through the tuning peg instead of through the bridge). Lock the string down with the appropriate Allen wrench, tool, or mechanism.

- Wind the string around the tuning peg as explained in tip #78.

- Adjust the string's fine-tuning knob so that it is as close to the middle of its range as you can determine. This gives you room to fine-tune the string later regardless of whether it goes sharp or flat. Often these knobs end up all the way at one end of their range shortly before a string breaks. This is because the string keeps stretching until it loses all its elasticity. In fact, when the fine-tuning knob runs out of room to tighten a flat string anymore, you might consider that a warning that the string may soon break.

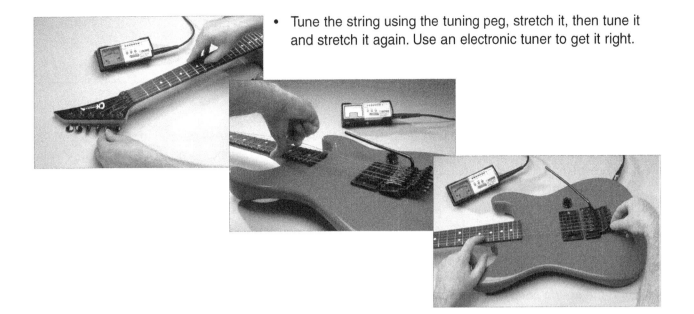

- Tune the string using the tuning peg, stretch it, then tune it and stretch it again. Use an electronic tuner to get it right.

- Lock that string back down at the nut if it's the only string you're changing. If you're changing all the strings (remember: one at a time), lock all the strings down at the nut after you've replaced them all.

If for some reason you must remove all the strings at once, plan on spending about an hour trying to get the balance back and the guitar in tune. Have some aspirin on hand and find a place to lie down for a while until the feelings of rage pass. If you find yourself in this predicament, wedge something strong under the back of the bridge assembly, in a position to prevent the bridge from pulling backward into the body cavity it rests in. (There are devices specially made to serve as this wedge. Ask your local music store to get one for you.) Your goal is to cause the bridge to sit exactly parallel with the guitar body, when seen from the side, as it should when it's perfectly balanced between in-tune strings and springs (see tip #91).

What you wedge into place here depends on the dimensions of your tremolo system; they're all a little different. Also, be careful that you don't harm the finish on your guitar with your wedge. Put some kind of cloth under the wedge if possible. Be sure to keep an eye on the fulcrum points of the bridge, which may come out of position while you have all the strings off. When you're set up, put the new strings on, starting with the heaviest (the lightest strings could break if put on first); tune each string as you put them on, stretch them, and tune them again.

When you have all the new strings on and have the guitar close to in tune, you're ready for the almost-final tuning. Tune your high E string, then the B string, then the high E string again. Then tune the G string, the B string, and the high E string again. Then tune the D string, the G string, the B string, and the high E again. Continue until you've tuned all the strings, always returning to double check the higher strings, which go out of tune easier.

When done with the almost-final tuning, press down on the bridge handle to remove your wedge and prepare to have to do the actual final tuning before locking down the nut.

91 KEEP IT LEVEL

The goal of an in-tune floating tremolo equipped guitar is for the bridge to sit parallel to the surface of the body of the guitar. If you've got the guitar tuned up but the bridge is sitting on an angle, its performance will not be optimal. Also, your guitar's action may be higher or lower than it should be, it will go out of tune during bends, you may experience some fretting out, and you may frequently break strings. Follow these instructions to solve the problem:

- Very high action, poor tremolo performance, and strings going out of tune when bending are symptoms that your bridge is leaning too far forward toward the tuning pegs. To fix this, you'll need to tighten the screws that hold the springs to bring the bridge parallel. Slightly loosen all the strings first, turn the spring screws clockwise ¼ to ½ turn, and re-tune. Repeat this process until you've got the guitar in tune and the bridge parallel to the body.

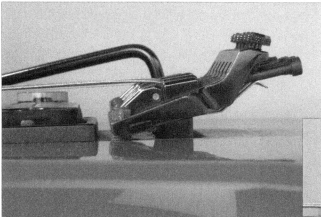

bridge leaning forward

bridge parallel

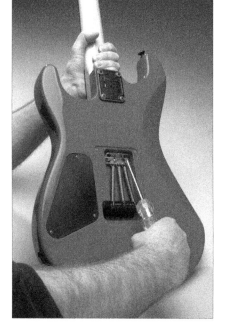

adjusting the springs

- Very low action, fretting out (fret buzz), poor tremolo performance, going out of tune when bending, and frequently breaking strings are a sign that your bridge is leaning too far backward into the body. To fix this and bring the bridge parallel you need to loosen the springs. Turn the screws counter-clockwise ¼ to ½ turn each, and re-tune. Don't worry about loosening your strings first; they'll detune and loosen as you loosen the spring screws a little. Repeat this process until you've got the guitar in tune and the bridge parallel to the body.

Here are a few additional floating bridge tips:

- Tremolo arm tension: On some models, you can simply turn the arm counter-clockwise to loosen it if you want it to hang free or clockwise to tighten it if you want it to stay put. On others, you'll need to use a small crescent or Allen wrench to loosen or tighten the nut and washers or the tension set screw on the underside of the bridge. You may have to remove the bridge from the guitar to do this. If you must make this adjustment, try doing so without taking off the strings. Loosen them just enough to get some slack in the springs, then remove the springs from the spring screws using a pair of vice grips. Wear eye protection when doing this procedure because the springs have a lot of tension on them and could suddenly and unexpectedly become dangerous projectiles. Then adjust your trem arm as necessary, re-attach the springs to the screws, and re-tune the guitar.

- Return your fine tuners to their mid-range as often as possible. Unclamp the nut locks, move the fine tuners to their middle position, tune the string with the tuning pegs, then clamp the nut locks back down. Do this frequently, so you'll always have the ability to tune either a sharp or flat string whenever necessary. The mechanics of any tremolo system could cause either situation at any time.

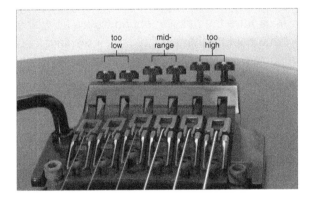

- Place a rubber band in the springs if necessary to reduce noise. Use a paper clip to thread the rubber bands through the springs.

- Use only three springs. Many floating bridge systems come with five springs in place. Most guitarists remove two and leave three, positioned so as to support the middle and both ends of the bridge block. Three springs should be plenty for optimal floating bridge performance. Five springs can make the tremolo system too tough to use, especially if you like to take deep dives.

- Keep a hand on the unplayed strings or on the tuning pegs to eliminate the crackling noise that may come through your amp when playing harmonics or using the tremolo. This noise is caused by the lack of grounding of the tremolo system. You'll have to act as the ground in these situations.

- Keep the bridge assembly clean and lubricated for best performance. Also, the frequent breaking of strings could be a sign that you need to replace cracked saddle inserts or that your nut is installed improperly (probably sideways).

- Determine the exact size of any of the small Allen wrenches needed to operate or maintain the tremolo system, then buy a half dozen of them at your local hardware store. They used to cost a whopping 50 cents each when I needed them. They're easily lost or stripped, so just buy a bunch right from the start, and you'll always have one around.

93 MIKING AMPS IN THE STUDIO

Almost any microphone will do in a pinch, but the classic guitar recording setup, used since the beginning of time (or at least since many of the classic rock albums of the sixties), involves a guitar speaker cabinet and a Shure SM-57 microphone. The tonal characteristics of this microphone work perfectly to best capture the frequencies emitted by guitar speaker cabs.

Most studio engineers place the mic close to the grill cloth—anywhere from touching the cloth to a foot away, based on personal preference. In general, most recording pros will point the mic straight into the speaker or at a slight downward angle and usually off center from the speaker cone. If you look at each individual speaker in the cabinet as a clock, most engineers will place the microphone at about two o'clock. The lower you go, the more bass you capture.

Allman Brothers Band producer Tom Dowd told me he often sets up and points microphones perpendicular to the speaker cabinet, instead of pointing them directly at the speaker. Dowd says this positioning will capture the passing sound waves as well as straight-in mic placement, but avoids having the microphone capture the "pop" of the air displacement caused by the moving speaker. That's how Dowd has recorded many of his classic albums dating back to 1947.

And of course, most engineers will place a second mic (often a condenser microphone) three or four feet away from the speaker cabinet and about four feet off the ground, pointed toward the sound source, to capture more of the "room" sound. The two signals can then be mixed together for a bigger sound. The room mic offers a bit of reverb and delay, as our ears would normally hear in a room with a raging amp. The close mic gives us the "punch"—the tight, crisp sound that really cuts through on our recordings.

When you listen to playback, put the sound through the studio's big speakers, plenty loud. Follow these simple steps in any electric guitar recording situation, and you'll capture your best sound.

mic straight at speaker
(second mic 3-4 ft. away)

Tom Dowd suggestion

Pete Anderson, producer and guitarist for country star Dwight Yoakam, has recorded a string of multi-platinum hits featuring acoustic guitar. Pete told me his method of miking acoustics is pretty simple: point a condenser mic at the guitar, from slightly behind and below the bridge and pointing up toward the bridge about 12 inches from the guitar. Acoustic guitars are a little like drums, and the bridge is at the center of the drum. The sound of an acoustic guitar actually comes from the vibrating wooden top of the guitar—not from the soundhole as one might think. The closer you place your microphone to the soundhole, the more fret noise you'll pick up.

Also, when miking a 12-string or an acoustic slide guitar—or a really clean, accurate player who doesn't make a lot of fret noise—Pete suggests pointing a condenser mic at the guitar between the strumming hand and the fretboard about 10 inches away. For resonator guitars, he suggests pointing the microphone at the resonator cone, away from the banging and clanging of the picking hand and slide. The resonator cone acts exactly like a speaker and, properly miked, will sound better than will the guitar's on-board pickup (if it has one).

acoustic

12-string

95 SAVE YOUR STUDIO EARS

So you've laid down some serious cash to cut tracks in a big-time recording studio. Now you've been out there in the big room with a pair of cans on your head, playing the same song for what seems like days. Your ears feel like they're on fire, and you're more than a little burned out. You're going deaf standing next to your fully cranked speaker cabinet, you feel like a bug in a jar on the lonely side of the control room window, and you're sick of communicating in clipped off phrases and sign language.

AC/DC guitar tech Geoff Banks told me that Angus Young—well known for high-volume guitar antics—runs a cable from his speaker cabinet into the recording studio control room, where he, his guitar, and his amp head can work comfortably for hours at a time while the speakers blare at 10 in the next room. No earaches; no clipped off, delayed conversations with the engineer and producer; and no more sign language. Save your studio ears and your sanity. Run the cable.

96 HOME RECORDING NECESSITIES

With the boom in home recording and the plethora of inexpensive recording gear available these days, many of us have opted to record our demos and CDs in the comfort of our own homes. The first piece of gear we all usually buy is the recording unit (or recording software) that allows us to lay down the most tracks possible within our budgets. The next piece of gear you simply must scrimp and save for, however, is the best mic pre-amp and, if you're doing digital recording, the best DA/AD (Digital to Analog/Analog to Digital) converter you can afford—even if it means an excruciating months-long wait before your piggy bank is fat enough for the purchase.

Why not buy the economy brands? Joe Satriani explained it to me this way: A digital recorder needs a certain quality signal to output the best possible sound in the finished product. Give it less than it needs and it has to fill in part of the signal, actually making up parts of the full frequency range it thinks you intended to send it.

A high-quality mic pre will output a signal that is as close to your guitar's real tonal characteristics as possible. Lower quality gear will, again, have to make up part of the signal. And the guesswork will be repeated again during the DA/AD part of the recording process, unless you're using the highest quality DA/AD converter you can get your hands on. Remember too, you can often rent this stuff by the day or week from a local music store or anywhere that recording or PA equipment is sold.

97 EFFECTS AND BAND SIZE

When you're playing in a large band, particularly if you've got keyboards or horn players on stage with you, you'll sometimes have a hard time "cutting through." And of course when you're playing in a three-piece (or even for acoustic players in a duo or solo setting), you may wish you were making a bigger, broader sound to make up for the fact that you don't have a second guitarist, keyboardist, or horn player beefing up your mix.

That's where effects pedals—or the lack of effects pedals—come in. When you're doing the trio thing (guitar, bass, drums) and/or duo or solo acoustic, you might want to add some reverb, chorus, delay, flanging, tremolo, or phase shifting—as well as (possibly) some overdrive or distortion—to fatten up the guitar and the group's overall sound.

When you're in a larger group setting, however, you need to keep your sound cleaner in order to cut through the clutter of all those frequencies emanating from your fellow musicians. It's the exact opposite situation from the small group setting, and chorus, delay, flanging, reverb—and sometimes even distortion or overdrive—will quickly cause you to be lost in the mix. Also, if you're playing with a keyboard player who is using chorus or delay, adding the same effects to the guitar will make the whole band sound muddy. Play it clean and crisp in a large group, and you'll be heard just fine.

98 CUT THROUGH ON SOLOS

Pedals and stomp boxes can boost your volume to help you cut through during a solo. But what if you're already using a distortion pedal, and it's on all the time? You could follow the advice in tip #29, or you could just add *another* pedal to your chain of effects—such as a second distortion pedal, an overdrive pedal, an equalizer, or a compressor.

If you opt for the two-pedal solution, use the first pedal in the chain primarily to boost the gain of the signal by setting its level (volume) higher and its drive (effect) lower. Use the second pedal to add the crunch, overdrive, or distortion by setting it as you would normally. Also note that an equalizer pedal has the added benefit of allowing you to boost or cut specific frequencies to better emphasize your preferred tonal characteristics.

99 SPEAKER PLACEMENT AT A GIG

In the effort to better hear ourselves, we often place our speakers, especially when we're using a combo amp, on top of another amp, chair, table, or anything we can fit it on. Do that if you must, but understand that you're losing precious low-end when you lift the speakers off the floor. It's better to just tilt your amp up so you can hear it than to lift it off the ground and lose your bottom entirely.

 100 ELIMINATE HUM

Almost all amplified rigs have a little hum, but excessive, annoying levels of hum are usually the result of the improper grounding of your amp or playing a guitar without humbucking pickups—such as a vintage Strat or Tele—close to fluorescent lights (even if they're off), computer monitors, televisions, neon lights or signs, and sometimes bar or restaurant refrigerators, ice machines, etc. Even regular stage lighting can cause hum if they're on the same power circuit as your amp or PA. If none of these scenarios describe your situation, you may need to open up your guitar (or have a qualified tech do it for you) and check potential ground trouble spots inside. There are a couple of easy solutions to the first two problems—easy for some people in some situations, that is. However, tearing into your guitar to solve internal ground problems is more complicated and beyond the scope of this book (but any good guitar repair and maintenance book will have answers for you).

Let's tackle what we can. If you're playing one of those single-coiled darlings in one of the above mentioned scenarios (and my heart goes out to you if the stage lighting consists solely of those awful office-style fluorescent bulbs, or just a couple of neon beer signs), you may have no choice but to change guitars—if you have a backup with humbuckers. Or, you'll have to quickly become very adept at turning your guitar's volume knob to zero any time you aren't playing. This becomes a job in itself, so if you're going to play that venue again, you might now become motivated to get a second job so you can pick up a Les Paul or other humbucker-equipped axe. If the hum appears to be coming strictly from your amp and is not caused by an internal problem within your guitar, you might simply be able to flick the ground switch on your amplifier to the opposite setting and resolve the issue. If your amp has no ground switch, you can try plugging the amplifier into a different electrical outlet—and here is where that 25-foot extension cord I told you to put in your toolbox (in tip #70) comes in handy. Sometimes it helps to reposition your amp or yourself. Changing the angle of your pickups relative to your amp can help. Any of these changes may reduce or eliminate that obnoxious hum.

 101 STOP MICROPHONE SHOCK

Microphone zaps are no fun. If you get shocked every time you step up to sing and play, try flicking your amp's ground switch the other direction. If that doesn't work, or if you don't have a ground switch on your amp, then the low-tech solution may be the best. Make it a habit of carrying a windscreen with you that you can slip over a mic when needed. This will keep you from making direct contact with the mic and therefore prevent the very surprising, painful, and mind-numbing shocks.